Tradie LADIES

Imogen Pershouse

Published in Australia by Silverbird Publishing Pty Ltd.

First published in Australia 2025
This edition published 2025
Copyright © Imogen Pershouse 2025
Cover design, typesetting: WorkingType (www.workingtype.com.au)

The right of Imogen Pershouse to be identified as the
Author of the Work has been asserted in accordance with the
Copyright, Designs and Patents Act 1988.

This book is a work of fiction. Any correlation to
any real individuals or institutions is purely coincidental.

ISBN: 978-1-923439-02-3

About the Author

Imogen Pershouse is the pseudonym of a nurse who has worked forty-two years full-time in rural and tertiary hospitals in Queensland and New South Wales. Her experiences in general, midwifery and intensive care nursing are used in her writing.

Tradie Ladies is her third book of medical biological fiction.

Other titles by Imogen Pershouse

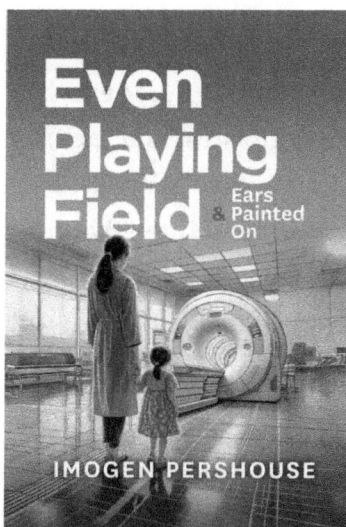

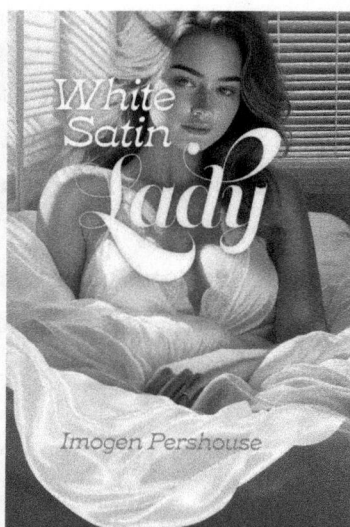

Even Playing Field,
Sid Harta,
ISBN: 978- 1-92295-8853

White Satin Lady,
Sid Harta,
ISBN: 978-1-923439-04-7

I am indebted to all those who helped me get this book published. A special thanks to Percy, Viv, Jimo, Glyn, Lillian, Keith, Jeff, Kay, Kerry Collison, Marie Pietersz, Susan Pierotti and Luke Harris.

Contents

One   Ants, ants and more ants!   1

Two   Jack's jeopardy   4

Three   Lazy Alice   14

Four   ICU night shift   19

Five   Smiley Kylie   28

Six   Sally's magnetism   50

Seven   The tradie ladies   56

Eight   Young's syndrome   66

Nine   Taylor's identity struggle   75

Ten   Kylie and Taylor   83

Eleven   Sally and Greg   94

Twelve   Becoming a new couple   110

Thirteen   Kylie's hesitation   124

Fourteen   Sally scalded   138

Fifteen   Embarrassed Sally   150

Sixteen	*Meeting Greg's parents*	174
Seventeen	*Kylie's spiritual dimensions*	181
Eighteen	*Meeting next of kin*	189
Nineteen	*Taylor's growing family*	201
Twenty	*Alice's malice*	211
Twenty-one	*Lilly*	217
Twenty-two	*Jack*	230
Twenty-three	*Taylor's departure*	236
Twenty-four	*Greg*	243
Twenty-five	*The importance of a living blood relative*	250
Twenty-six	*The score card*	252
Twenty-seven	*Jack's endless love*	257
Twenty-eight	*Everyone home*	262

Chapter One

Ants, ants and more ants!

*J*ack Robinson was found cold, unconscious and barely alive. Black ants were exiting his nose, ears, eyes and every other body orifice. When found covered in leaves and dirt, despite it being summer, Jack's core temperature was only 28 degrees Celsius. The attending ambulance paramedic immediately wrapped him in a foil heat reflective blanket to prevent further heat loss.

In the frantic Emergency Department, Jack's body was resuscitated from hypothermia with warmed intravenous and bladder fluids instilled immediately. He was also intubated and ventilated with heated ventilated gases to aggressively restore his core body temperature to over 32 degrees. After his peripheral blood flow was restored, Jack's thin pale body began shivering violently. The electric thermal blanket blew warm air onto his body to prevent rebound cooling. The sheepskin situated between Jack's body and the firm hospital mattress provided further insulation from heat loss. Although most of the ants had been killed with insecticide sprayed on the white ironed sheets, a few periodically migrated from Jack's anus, penis and nostrils where the bite marks were most severe.

Jack's son, Taylor, a special forces soldier, was exhausted after flying home overnight from a confidential military mission. At twenty-eight years old, he was 183 cm tall, had dark curly hair and was tanned, solid and muscular. His compact frame presented a stark contrast to his frail father's hollowed orbital ridges, freckled, wrinkled dry skin and soft sinewy hands. Jack's pathological stillness amplified the visual effects of his advanced age and fragility. Jet-lagged but unable to rest before seeing his critically ill father, sleep deprived Taylor prioritised his Intensive Care Unit (ICU) visit before returning to his childhood home.

Withering from fatigue and walking on autopilot, he stopped in his tracks abruptly, surprised to find a teary, petite female bending over, talking to his father. The young lady was holding his hands under the blanket. Instinctively trained in stealth and to be a lethal force, Taylor moved closer to hear the young female's dialogue with his unconscious father.

'I'm so sorry, Jack,' the sobbing lady said. 'I should

never have listened to you. This is all my fault ... I should have trusted my instincts.'

'What did you do to my father?' Taylor angrily demanded, standing rigidly with his hand on his hips. Too tired to display any tact or subtlety, Taylor persisted with his queries despite no answers forthcoming. 'How did this happen? Who are you?'

Alarmed at his impatience, Kylie's reddened blue eyes and clumped dark eyelashes diverted from Jack's face. She looked up in dismay at a scowling soldier looming menacingly over her. Her flushed sodden face, portraying guilt, gazed intently at the angry green eyes and heavily creased frown. With her mouth gaping open, Kylie was rendered dumbstruck at the sight of a soldier wearing a khaki and light brown camouflage operational combat uniform. Kylie froze. Her tears continued streaming down her pale face to spot her pale pink blouse. Her grief was instantly replaced with shock and confusion. The soldier's jaw muscles twitched and tightened. His lips compressed again in frustration when no answers came.

'I repeat, what did you do to my father!' the irate young soldier demanded in a testosterone-filled response. He widened his foot stance and folded his honed muscled arms across his broad chest in confrontation.

Chapter Two
Jack's jeopardy

*N*ormally in a combative stance, Taylor would take his opponent down. With none of his questions answered, however, he found himself in quite a predicament. The pretty one had attempted to flee. When Taylor moved to obstruct her flight, she had ended up with her face buried in his sternum with her sobbing reignited.

Taylor foolishly found himself embracing this vulnerable stranger, unable to determine whether she was friend or foe. He'd instinctively known she was about to bolt when she'd released his father's hand, buried under the warming blanket, to look around. Who was she? Why couldn't she answer a straight question? What was she apologising for? Taylor was used to his troops obeying commands. Confused by her reactions as he held her captive, Taylor found himself embracing her, unsure whether it was the right tactic. From a brief observation, it did not look as though this delicate creature had intended his father any harm. Did he look so terrifying that he'd forced her to try to flee in fear?

Taylor had phoned ICU during his flights. Somewhere in the back of his mind, he now seemed to recall the nurses reassuring him that Jack was not alone. Someone called Kylie had sat beside his father's bed all night. Yet when confronted, the sad female had slammed into the firm wall of Taylor's chest as he'd instinctively blocked her path. Now that Taylor had successfully contained this soft body entrapped in his arms, what was he to do with her? Withering with fatigue, Taylor found himself unsure how to proceed. Years of working in a structured disciplined male unit had left him feeling an awkward sense of intrigue and fascination towards this floral-scented feminine bundle.

'Mr Robinson?' a doctor tentatively asked as he approached.

'Yes,' Taylor responded, his reflexes automatically releasing his "prey". Taylor turned, holding out his hand to the new distraction introducing himself.

'I am Doctor John O'Brien, tonight's ICU resident. I was just called by the nurses to update you on your father's progress and test results. Shall we all go into the interview room?' the doctor suggested, his arms outstretched, indicating the direction. 'I'd also like to get some information from you both on Jack's normal functioning and cognitive status.' Indicating the automated machine, he invited, 'Would anyone like a coffee, tea or cold drink before we begin?'

'No, I'm fine, thanks,' said Taylor.

'I'm fine, too,' said Kylie.

'Well,' Dr O'Brien began, 'I will start with the CAT scan. Jack fractured his frontal skull bone during his fall,' the doctor stated, pointing to his forehead. 'As you saw, a ventilator is keeping Jack's airway clear and maintaining his normal ventilation. The ventilator also helps Jack's brain swelling, which we call cerebral oedema, to resolve. The ventilator gases have warmed Jack's core temperature gradually after he was found unconscious with hypothermia, lying on pieces of broken bricks and large rocks under his neighbour's house. He arrived covered in leaves, dirt and ants. As Jack's temperature improved and we were able to start cleaning him up, we found several large pus-filled wounds on his back from the sustained pressure of the bricks he had been lying on. Jack is also covered in ant bites.'

'What was he doing under the Samuels' house?' asked Taylor, confused.

Kylie swallowed before interjecting hesitantly. 'Unfortunately, Jack was developing short-term memory loss. Hoping the cause might be something treatable like an infection, about a month ago, I organised a medical review, septic screen and blood work-up. The cognitive testing demonstrated the intermittent short-term memory loss pattern of early dementia that was likely to progress as Jack aged. This diagnosis indicated Jack was becoming a danger to himself. There were intermittent subtle clues, like Jack overlooking important things like turning off the stove. Occasionally, he was not remembering to take his medications from his blister packs; other times, he had forgotten to eat or lock his external doors. However, Jack was resistant to being placed in twenty-four-hour supervised care. After Jack pleaded with me for one last night at home, I got permission to delay his admission into long-term care for another day. The problem is that Jack's long-term memories are intact. He was reluctant to leave his beautiful home with all his happy memories of you and Michelle. Jack's eyes brightened up when he showed me items Michelle had made or when he talked about special family occas—'

'Why wasn't I notified?' Taylor interrupted. 'Surely I am down as Dad's next of kin?'

'I left several messages at an army military command post over several weeks when the diagnosis was made. I received no responses or returned calls.'

'I'm sorry. I didn't get any messages. I am in the special forces. I was stationed at a secret location for six months doing operational military defence manoeuvres.'

Taylor shook his head, wondering where the communication breakdown occurred.

Kylie continued. 'So, Jack was resisting moving into

what he referred to as "public accommodation". He was intent on staying in his own home, surrounded by his beautiful memories. Jack had begged me to give him one more night to pack. I had only reluctantly agreed after Jack and I had compiled a list of what he wanted to pack. I had offered to do the packing for Jack because he was oblivious of his cognitive deficits. Dr James, the gerontologist, had explained to him that his short-term memory was failing, making it unsafe for him to drive his car and cook. However, since Jack did not remember the conversation, he was agitated because he believed the decision was being made without his consultation. Jack had no insight into our safety concerns. Therefore, under the Mental Health Act and our professional duty of care, we needed to protect Jack by providing twenty-four-hour residential care.'

'I would have hired a nurse to reside with Dad in our home if I had known. I do not want Dad living where he is unhappy,' Taylor asserted.

'I wish I had been able to contact you on the number on the file. I tried several times without any success. None of my calls were returned. If you did speak to Jack, he might not have recalled our need to contact you. I had also hoped you might call when I was there.'

'Well, if Dad survives this, that is the arrangement we will make. I want Dad to stay at home with supervised care, please,' Taylor adamantly insisted.

'We will discuss those arrangements if we can when

Jack is out of ICU. He will need reassessing again after the skull fracture heals,' Dr O'Brien suggested. 'There are many variables here, Taylor. We are unsure when Jack fractured his skull. There were other insults on his brain too, like the low temperature exposure and an acidosis from his shallow breathing while unconscious. We cannot do any cognitive assessments until Jack is no longer sedated or needing analgesics infused. We have no idea how long he was unconscious or whether he has cognitively deteriorated due to a lack of oxygen and impaired ventilation. We need to do further neurological assessments after we wake him up. However, we cannot wake him up until the brain swelling resolves. For his age, Jack's kidneys and liver are functioning reasonably well. We are not supporting his blood pressure or heart function at this stage. We are just providing mechanical ventilation, sedation, antibiotics, fluids and calories.'

Sighing deeply, Taylor raked his thick, curly hair while stretching back in the solid navy fabric chair. 'That is such a relief, Doctor. Thank you so much for your care. Were the police called to look for Dad?'

'Yes,' Kylie intervened. 'Within one hour of Jack not answering the door, I'd rung my supervisor and the police. We searched his backyard and walked along the footpath and both sides of the street. We talked to neighbours while we waited for the locksmith to permit entry to Jack's house for a wellbeing check. We also checked the local shops, his doctor's surgery and the places of his usual activities, like the neighbourhood lawn bowls centre. I did not realise, until Jack was found, that the note we found next to the alarm clock in the kitchen was Jack setting an alarm to sound for 10.45 am. That time was fifteen minutes before I was due to arrive. After I left, Jack must have written himself a Post-it note to set his alarm clock to sound before I was due to arrive the next day. Jack seems to have made his way under the neighbour's house, planning to hide there. It seems as though Jack's scheme failed when he tripped over the rubble on the uneven ground in the dark. Since Jack usually set alarms to remember appointments, we thought he might have planned to go somewhere. Jack had agreed that after one more night at home, he would consent to being admitted to the nursing home for twenty-four-hour supervision. I had got into a habit of checking on Jack on my way home after looking after my other patients' hygiene cares and dressings.'

'So, when had you last seen Dad?' Taylor chided, trying to remain calm.

'I did his leg ulcer dressing after his shower Monday morning at 11 am. Then Monday evening, on my way home at 5 pm, I popped in to heat up Jack's evening meal in the microwave for him. I turned on his television for the quiz show he enjoys, as it was beginning about 5.05 pm. At about 5.15, Jack walked me out as I was leaving. I stayed outside until I heard him lock the door behind me. I was worried that Jack had not begun packing. Jack had assured me by holding up the list on the table that he would get to it in the morning. So, when Jack did not answer the door, I was immediately concerned. Jack usually answers the door and phone promptly. I was alarmed when neither was answered.'

'When was Dad found?'

'Tuesday evening, just before 8 pm. Apparently the Samuels' dog was barking so incessantly that they went outside several times, looking for an intruder. Jack had climbed under their house, on the side that was fenced off from the dog. Their beige labrador was anxiously pawing at the ground, barking and wagging his tail so dramatically that the Samuels went inside again to get a torch. I had notified them that Jack was missing and had left my contact details. They found Jack cold, unconscious and partially covered in leaves from a nearby deciduous tree on that side of the house.'

'If Dad climbed under the house at 11 am, he had only been missing for about nine hours! No wonder he was so cold. Dad's pretty thin these days.'

'Yes, he is.' Dr O'Brien and Kylie nodded in agreement.

'Nine hours of deterioration can be a long time for Jack's age! I had tried daily to convince Jack about his need for residential care for his own safety. But the problem with intermittent short-term memory loss is that Jack often had no awareness of his deficit. When I could not contact you, I was getting increasingly anxious. I even rang Jack on the weekends and drove past to check him when I was not at work. Jack remained very resistant about moving. Retrospectively, I should have been suspicious when he suddenly agreed to move after one last night at home. I had convinced myself that Jack finally understood my concerns. Jack had even helped me write the list of items he was intending to pack and had placed three photo frames on the table ready.'

'Would you say Jack mobilised independently, then?' asked Dr O'Brien, keen to gain an understanding of Jack's pre-admission abilities.

'Yes, Jack's lower back arthritis ached at times, but he was tidy and independent. Occasionally, Jack got dizzy if he changed his position too quickly, like if he put his head back to rinse his hair after a shampoo. I showered him sitting on a sturdy plastic chair and washed his feet to save him bending. Jack mostly ate the pre-made, nutritionally balanced meals purchased from the supermarket, after I heated them up for him in the microwave. Prior to the leg ulcer forming three months ago, Jack had mowed the lawn himself and had done his own cordless vacuuming. However, we decided to send house cleaning services and lawn maintenance teams to Jack's house to encourage leg elevation for wound healing. The cleaners kept the fridge, microwave and bathroom hygienic. Jack had agreed to all those services coming to him provided he could stay home. We had already delayed Jack's transfer longer than we wanted to. Jack was waiting to hear from you.'

Kylie elaborated further. 'Jack's fond long-term memories are remarkable. He recalls his wife, Michelle, losing her battle with bowel cancer. Jack can show you the curtains with colourful butterflies and birds Michelle made on her sewing machine, the skilfully embroidered teddy bears with ribbon love hearts on the lounge cushions and the walled tapestries of tigers, poodles and horses framed on the lounge walls. He was very adamant about not leaving this personalised haven he'd lived in for sixty years for bland almond-coloured nursing home walls.'

Kylie listed her ongoing concerns. 'At 180 cm tall, Jack weighed only 65 kg. With his short-term memory loss, he was not remembering the names of people or items. Sometimes, Jack was becoming confused and indecisive in simple tasks like choosing his groceries. So, I hid his car keys to stop him driving. I was rostered to dress Jack's leg ulcer every second day after I assisted him to shower. Economically, the elderly are usually permitted to remain at home until it costs seventy-five per cent of the cost of residential accommodation to support them. However, in Jack's case, it was unsafe for him to live alone. Jack has always been a kind and courteous gentleman, even though he was very unhappy about the gerontology team decision to relocate him.'

Chapter Three
Lazy Alice

*I*n ICU, the 180-cm-tall night duty nurse Greg leaned over the navy vinyl and wood designed desk talking to his team leader, Sally, on the other side of the nursing station. Looking behind Sally, he observed Alice who had just returned from maternity leave and had finished her eight-hour shift. Alice was covertly stealing some of the ICU stores of toilet paper and tissues before heading home.

'The meek might inherit the earth, but they won't have it for long,' Greg asserted.

Sally looked over her shoulder at Alice furtively leaving the utility room, carrying the bag of stolen hospital supplies, before shaking her head disapprovingly.

'Alice possesses the ethics of an alley cat. Her gall never ceases to amaze me. She's as lazy as a fart in bed. The physiotherapist told me last week that one of her ventilated patients sustained a leg nerve palsy after she had failed to reposition him for an entire twelve-hour shift. Alice frustrates the hell out of me. She spends more time fabricating excuses than delivering professional standards of care.'

'Yes, exactly,' replied handsome Greg. 'I hate working with her. One night, Alice actually pulled the drawers out from the desk to drape her legs over them. She was supposed to be looking after a ventilated patient. Helen, who was busy working with her unstable ventilated patient at the next bed space, got really fed up with Alice ignoring her patient's alarms. Helen got so furious that she stormed over to the desk. With her hands on her hips and a disdainful withering look, she demanded Alice watch her ventilated patient from the bed area and respond to her own bloody alarms.'

'It is ridiculous that you have to demand that a supposedly qualified Registered Nurse do their bloody job! She's beyond morally dubious. I doubt she actually possesses a conscience. Leaving a ventilated patient out of your eyesight is negligent.'

'I totally agree. How can she accept a professional wage for putting in such minimal effort? It feels like she only comes to work to steal crucial patient resources.'

'Yes, the only effort she exerts is sucking up to management for protection.'

'Well ... most of us have had a gutful.'

'Joan suggested that Alice should be given a team

review so her colleagues can provide feedback on how her behaviours affect them.'

'Good luck with that! Alice gets negative feedback and disapproval from her colleagues every shift I work with her. She spends more energy generating pathetic excuses than improving her substandard performance.'

'Yeah, the doctors comment that Alice operates like a sociopath the way she lacks empathy and schemes to enslaves others. One evening, I actually saw Alice ring her mother up to bring up some stockings for her next shift. It was unbelievable to witness a selfish twenty-four-year-old nurse making her elderly mother run after her! Alice's mother babysits her granddaughter, allowing her to party all night. After Alice approached Rachel to move in with her "for company", she did no housework whatsoever. Rachel reckoned she was frightened to go to sleep, with Alice bringing different men home all hours of the day and night. Alice offered no money for board and was using up all her power, food and consumables without ever replacing anything. Rachel got so fed up with the parasitic relationship that she asked Alice to move out. Rachel now regrets having let Alice move in without setting boundaries.'

'Where does Alice's money go then?' Greg asked with a robotic shrug.

'Well, she drank three *bottles* of the free red wine at the last conference.'

'You're kidding me?'

'No, unfortunately I am not. Then, she boasted of sleeping with one of the younger doctors.'

'Has Alice always been like that?'

'If you mean completely self-absorbed, yes! For as long as she's worked here, anyway.' Sally's lip involuntarily curled in disgust.

'Then, we do need to have a team review to get Alice back on track, for her own sake as well as for patient safety.'

'I doubt it will work! Alice will lash out by diverting attention away from herself by criticising or abusing others rather than accept accountability for her actions.'

'I expect you're right there. But we should at least try to enforce professional standards because the patients allocated to her are vulnerable. It's not just the unit's reputation: we cannot keep ordering stores after every shift she works to replace the stock she is blatantly stealing. Maybe we should ring security as she is leaving?'

'Yes, ring security now. That is safer than Alice retaliating with power games. Most of us have confronted her about her stealing, but Alice then gets defensive and aggressive because she feels so entitled. Being caught by security could be the wake-up call she needs.'

'Hospital security need to catch her red-handed in the hospital grounds,' Sally said as she rang security, notifying them that Alice was headed down to the back car park with stolen hospital property. 'I've had that thought too late. Alice is most likely gone by now.'

'Won't it be good to get home today,' Greg considered. 'All we have done this shift is warm Jack, stabilise his vital signs, photograph and dress his wounds and bites and scrub the dirt off one exposed body part at a time ... and kill ants all night.'

Greg placed Jack's morning bloods in the '"courier out"' basket before returning to the bedside. Sally came around the desk to assist Greg label the photographs of all the wounds and bites with their sites, dates and times.

'At least we have achieved getting his core temperature to thirty-three degrees. Now Jack's body temperature is correcting, his clotting enzymes will begin functioning. Clearing his airway is resolving his acidosis too,' Greg mentioned, looking at the arterial blood gas results.

'When we start to wake him up, though, the nightmare could begin! Jack's dementia and fractured skull might make it challenging to keep his lines and tubes in.'

'That will be next week's problem after his cerebral oedema resolves.'

Chapter Four

ICU night shift

'*I*’ve asked for you to run between the nurses with ventilated patients tonight, Greg, after your huge workload last night.'

'Thanks, Sally. I appreciate the thoughtfulness. It was a twelve-hour marathon, wasn't it?'

'Yeah. Hopefully, tonight might have more routine cases. I also want a more experienced nurse on the floor to support the juniors while I attend the ward medical emergencies. Our skill mix tonight is not so great. After three recent retirements, we have more novices rostered on than experienced staff.'

'Sure, no problem.'

On seeing a flurry of activity outside the Emergency Department, Greg moved to the window to look.

'I wonder what that is all about.'

As Sally looked out the window down to the ambulance

parking bay, the officers were standing back, hosing off an ambulance gurney with a high-pressure spray.

'Might've been a deceased arriving for confirmation of death?' Greg rationalised.

'Or someone's vomited or been incontinent? Could be a multi-trauma with blood and glass everywhere.'

The desk phone rang. Sally as team leader answered the call, looking sympathetically towards Greg, who would need to take the new admission. Greg collected a ventilator to set up after Sally pointed to bay five, raising her hand in a "V for ventilator" sign. Sally continued busily scribbling all the information she was given.

'Gosh, Greg! We've had no infestations for about five years, and now we get them two nights in a row!'

'That's okay. What have we got?'

'I can swap the staff around if you want.'

'No, we will manage. What's on the way?'

'The new admission is Joe Stanley, a sixty-five-year-old with an extensive history of alcoholism. Joe was found collapsed on his back stairs with a temperature of 30.6 degrees. He has been incontinent of urine and faeces. From their observations of the scene, the ambulance officers believe that Joe had diarrhoea and slipped in his own excreta while descending the stairs. Joe has a large contusion on the occipital ridge at the back of his head, most likely from the impact of his head hitting the stairs behind him as he fell. When the ambulance went to check Joe's kitchen and bedroom for his medications, they were overwhelmed by a foul stench. Investigating the strong odour, they found bottles and buckets filled with urine everywhere inside the house. I am so sorry, Greg! This unkempt gent is apparently covered in faecal fluid and maggots. I will help you get him sorted as much as I can.'

'I am going to wear insecticide instead of deodorant for my next shift, I swear!' Greg joked. 'What are the chances of having two patients with live bugs coming out every body orifice two nights in a row?'

'Ants and maggots, I can do; spiders, no way! No matter the size or the type, spiders are just *tooooo* much.'

'I wouldn't have picked you as arachnophobic,' Greg teased. 'Remember when I was orientating on my first day in the ICU? Before Alice could introduce me to you, you suddenly squealed and jumped back. A small live huntsman spider fell out of the box as you got the Christmas decorations down off the lockers. I watched you leap for the insecticide and drown it in spray, well after it was beyond resuscitation. The spider was paralysed with its legs folded underneath, unable to gain traction to move. You were stooped forward, still spraying. Even when we were being introduced, you barely moved your eyes off it. Do you remember me getting a paper towel to scoop it into the bin?'

'Yes, well ... I appreciated your effort! Spiders should not exist on this planet,' Sally insisted.

Greg recalled how flushed Sally was. She had looked so cute. Her sapphire eyes were fixated and deadly serious, watching the inert spider as though it might reincarnate. Since their first introduction eighteen months ago, as much as Greg tried to treat Sally as a colleague, he had struggled. Every single shift they had worked together, Greg was magnetised by the gorgeous hue in those expressive blue eyes. Even now, with half her face hidden under her mask, checking the bedside emergency equipment was operational, Sally's elegant small frame made her look beyond pretty.

After looking away helplessly, Greg's eyes soon returned to admire Sally's smooth tanned skin and round buns. Greg chatted, intermittently looking up from the prescribed ventilator settings he was programming into the machine. Thank God his body's reaction was hidden under a protective gown. Lately, Greg had taken to wearing plastic aprons automatically whenever Sally was around. The more he got to know Sally, the worse his attraction grew. Greg was entranced by her graceful mannerisms and impressed by her intelligence. He loved her soft, articulate voice and her gorgeous face. A besotted fool! With Sally never attending any ICU parties, he was pinning all his hopes of spending time with her on this year's ICU scientific conference.

Emergency nurse Sonya arrived, escorting the offensive smelling Joe on an emergency trolley. Sonya apologised for Joe's filthy state.

'We had to get out the sponge bowl just to clean a space to place the blood pressure cuff and apply a finger probe for his oxygen saturation measurements. Joe will need a thorough scrub before you can insert an arterial line and central line in his heart when his temperature and clotting times improve. When we checked Joe's back for pressure areas, we gave him a quick wash, but the diarrhoea has been non-stop. We can't even put an anal tube in to contain his fluid faecal soiling until his temperature corrects and the clotting enzymes are functional. With Joe's temperature so low, we have the ventilator humidifier raising his core temperature up to 37 degrees.'

Several incontinence sheets were placed over the new bed linen, under Joe. As they transferred the dishevelled Joe onto an ICU bed from the emergency trolley, the smell invading Sally's nostrils caused her to dry heave. The sight of so many white wriggling maggots did not help. Before his arrival, Sally had just devoured a muesli bar with white rice and coconut shreds. The rice and coconut had looked disgustingly similar to those writhing white grubs. Trying to control her imagination, Sally put on double gloves only to tear the top glove and feel a wiggling maggot vibrating between the latex layers. Rubbish bins and insecticide spray were brought closer to the bed to remove the very mobile maggots. Greg laughed, uninhibited – a fat wriggling maggot was outpacing his finger's attempt to remove it.

'Look at the fat little bugger move. You could throw a saddle on him,' he bantered, trying to amuse and distract his retching team leader.

Unable to help herself, Sally looked down and laughed. 'Oh, God help us!'

Sally's look of disgust was followed by an involuntary shiver, as though she was maxed. Holding her breath frequently, Sally looked intent on maintaining her professional facade.

'You're just lucky,' Greg provoked. 'Not every chick I spend a night with gets such unique experiences as this.'

Sally couldn't help but laugh. The combined impact of the faecal stench, the visual cue of so many fleeing maggots, the reeking unkempt patient and night duty fatigue invaded her mind. Another finger with a torn glove buzzed from the vibration of live maggots wriggling between the layers. Sally folded the gloves over on themselves as she removed them, trying to contain the mobile maggots in the torn latex. Cringing involuntarily, she discarded both sets of gloves into the nearest plastic bag lined bin, spraying yet more insecticide.

'Well, let me tell you, Greg. If this is your idea of a stimulating evening, I understand why you are still single,' Sally taunted. 'While there is no doubt these nights may have been exciting and non-stop entertainment, I am not so sure that this is how to go about making an evening unforgettable!'

'Oh, you must admit, this is a good way to highlight my charm and charisma.'

'We'll agree that your attention to hygiene and citrus-scented cologne provides a sharp contrast, shall we?' Sally smiled cheekily under her mask, creasing the corners of her eyes as though entertained immensely.

'Definitely. I heard a female comedian once joke about partner preferences. The comedian said when she was young, she wanted her male partners tall, dark, lean and handsome. At middle age, she wanted them wealthy, intelligent and witty. In her senior years, she said she had to settle for them just possessing a pulse.'

Greg looked at the monitor, still displaying an erratic cardiac rhythm. Joe had been having self-limiting arrhythmias while the ventilator-humidified gases were warming him internally to a normal temperature. The informal bedside echo was showing the enlarged heart chambers of an alcohol-related cardiomyopathy.

'Oh, well, we are both still marketable by those standards,' Sally smirked.

'Speak for yourself, girl! I am still in phase one.'

Greg grinned, looking at Sally's amused, deep blue eyes glowing brightly under the fluorescent lights. Her short curly blonde hair fell forward on to her face and remained there. Sally kept her maggot-infested gloves covered in faecal fluid away from her face and body.

'Well, this is my last shift after working four nights in a row. So, I am in the third phase. I'm extremely grateful the ward Medical Emergency Team (MET) pager has not alarmed tonight and that my pillow is only four hours away. I am also glad that ICU has had no emergencies tonight, with our dubious skill mix. With these heavy workloads, my definition of success lately has diminished to just being able to get everyone off for their meal breaks and home on time.'

'Then you are settling for small mercies. You need more from life than that,' Greg insisted, watching Sally hopefully.

'Study, shiftwork and the daily crises here are all I can manage,' Sally sighed, exhibiting fatigue.

'Then come to watch the battle of the bands playing at the beach festival on Saturday night with me.'

'Aren't you exhausted for days after finishing your stints of nights?'

'I enjoy lifting my mood with music, a beer and good company.'

'I'm not sure that worrying about my science exams would classify me as good company.'

'Come on … just four hours. Have a night off! Break the cycle of sleep, eat, study and work. We can see who else in the unit might be interested too, if you like.'

Sally shrugged, uncertainly wondering whether Greg was asking her out on a date or if this was a group ICU invite.

Greg made eye contact, attempting to assess whether Sally was interested in going out with him. The last thing he needed was to divulge too much and piss off the team leader he was attracted to. Greg worried that his irresistible chemistry with Sally could complicate his work life. Always determined to keep his work and social lives separate, Greg had tried to pay attention to other females. However, he soon gave up when he recognised his heart was not in it. Like it or not, his yearning was exclusively for the slender beauty before him, socially distancing herself. Greg was as powerless to resist Sally as she seemed clueless about his interest in her.

Chapter Five

Smiley Kylie

*F*ollowing their conversation with Dr O'Brien, Taylor felt an unconventional need, for some reason, to apologise for startling her on his arrival. Frankly, he was disgusted with himself. What he had understood about her conversation with the doctor was that this professional nurse took her job seriously. How could he have upset her to the extent that she chose to escape rather than endure his condescending presence? Taylor had watched in awe as Kylie had articulated succinctly to the calm doctor. He intuitively realised his irritation was fuelled by tiredness, jet lag and anxiety.

'I would like to take you for a coffee and chat. Is that okay? I was very upset before at seeing Dad, looking ... near death.' When Kylie nodded, he continued. 'Could you wait another five minutes? I just want to give Dad a kiss and say hello before I leave. I've been travelling all day and most of the night.'

'How about I take you back to my place for the coffee? The spare room is made up and you can crash there without having to make your bed immediately.' Kylie invited. 'I am concerned there will be no groceries at Jack's. We haven't shopped this week. Jack's car battery is also likely to be flat, and the car may have no fuel.' Kylie elaborated, 'Jack would want me to look after you, too.'

'Wow, that is so kind!' Taylor rubbed both hands over his fatigued face and eyes.

'I feel very responsible for this outcome. I usually took Jack to the shops on Thursdays to stock up for the weekend. How about you have breakfast at my place and a sleep in the spare room? Then I can drop you home on my way to work tomorrow, or to the hospital – whichever you like.'

'Thank you. I am rather beat.' Taylor's large hand covered a prolonged yawn, before he rubbed his weary face again.

Kylie waited outside, giving Taylor time alone with Jack. When they left ICU, Taylor put his travel bag on the back seat of her car as instructed. Kylie's car looked organised, as though where he put his bag was reserved for groceries while the other side was arranged with nursing dressings and solutions. As they drove off, glancing over the back, Taylor was surprised to see a grinder and circular saw, partially covered by a blanket. Taylor tentatively folded his tall solid physique into Kylie's Honda CRV.

'Kylie, I really want to apologise to you again about my behaviour when I first arrived. I'm not myself at the moment.' Taylor's eyes misted over as his thoughts recalled Jack's vulnerable appearance.

'That's okay,' Kylie replied, defensively focusing on the traffic.

'No, it's not. My behaviour was not at all acceptable. I was so shocked. Dad looked so old and fragile. I was stressed seeing him attached to all those machines. He looked so pale ... thin ... near dead!'

'Yes, seeing him so depleted is stressful. Think no more of it. I haven't,' Kylie said, displaying her usual unrivalled patience.

Taylor's usually calm emotions were volatile. He felt guilty and concerned at how much his father had deteriorated in the last six months while he had been on this last mission. Jack was losing weight and obviously becoming more dependent.

'I'm probably too exhausted for reasoning right now, but I'm wondering what choices in the health care models will allow Dad to stay in his own home.'

'Yes, that was what I had wanted to talk to you about, actually,' Kylie mentioned.

'What do you suggest?'

'I wanted to ask your permission for me to stay there with your dad, sleeping in his spare room. Jack would still have to go into a supervised day care centre during the day while I was at work. My preference is to keep Jack in his own home as long as possible. Jack loves his home and memories so much that staying at home in familiar surroundings will keep him orientated and delay further dementia decline. You will probably notice when you go home that I have nailed up a wall clock in every room. There is a clock calendar with the day, date and time on his kitchen table too.'

'I would agree to that,' Taylor affirmed. 'I did not get your message. During military operations, we provide a dedicated number for family or important contacts. Our supervisors only relay urgent messages for security reasons, in case our enemies could get valuable personal information by monitoring our electronic traffic.'

'I did not know why you were not returning my calls, and Jack could not tell me where you were. I had actually hoped you might ring while I was at Jack's.'

'I still have not returned to my locker to get any messages. Sorry ... I cannot explain more about my role. All I can say is that I was uncontactable. How does this arrangement work?'

'My employers will request you to sign a standard liability waiver. It protects them from being sued should your dad fall or have an accident while under my care. The standard waiver protects them and me from liability in what is considered an ambiguous care situation. What that means is that I still get my usual maximum nursing hours allocated for Jack, to give him a shower and dress his ulcer; however, while I promise to take all care, I cannot be responsible if Jack falls or leaves the house while I am asleep or in the shower.'

'That is reasonable. I understand that Dad could fall or wander off again at any time. My priority is for Dad to stay home safely for as long as possible.'

'There are lots of clever tricks we can do to improve safety, like installing movement sensor lighting and putting special locks on the doors. We can attach bells to his slippers and his bedroom, front and back doors to help me detect unexpected movement. The cleaning and mowing services would still come. I can also cook, clean and tidy for your dad.'

'That would be fine. I think Dad would be pleased to have daytime activities with others while you are at work. It would be safer than him living alone.'

'When you come home on your holidays, I will return to my unit. That way, you both enjoy your time together. You would also need to coordinate your annual leave with mine or vice versa. When you come home, I would take my annual leave then, or another community nurse can relieve me.'

'I see. That is a good idea.'

Kylie flipped on her blinker and pulled into her duplex. After they both alighted from her vehicle, Kylie locked her car and opened the front door.

'Here we are. Make yourself at home,' Kylie said, pointing to the spare room. 'I will get you a towel for when you freshen up while I make coffee and breakfast. How does bacon and eggs sound?'

'Brilliant!'

Taylor followed Kylie to the spare room where she left him to store his luggage before showing him the location of her bathroom. As Kylie turned abruptly to leave the bathroom, she again found herself pleasantly embedded in the chest of the man mass obstructing her narrow exit.

'I'm sorry,' Kylie apologised, smiling. 'I am really clumsy, especially after being awake all night. Sometimes I can't get out of my own way, so don't expect me to get out of yours.'

Taylor smiled. As before, he found the unexpected contact with Kylie's soft, floral scented frame pleasant. She could do that as often as she wanted, he conceded.

As Taylor wandered back after his shower to the room barefooted, wearing shorts and a white T-shirt, Kylie's eyes widened. His appearance was a stark contrast to the military uniform implanted in her memory. Taylor watched intently as her eyes roamed from his honed pecs to his taut legs. Only the bacon spitting oil as it cooked seemed to break her reverie.

The enticing smell of bacon drifting in the unit and the previous sounds of their voices precipitated frantic scratching at the laundry door. As Kylie opened the door, an orangey-brown, furry little Pomeranian dog yapped excitedly. She circled frantically, before standing on her tiny hind legs, waiting expectantly for a pat. Kylie bent down to greet her exuberant pet.

'And this is Hayley. How are you, cheeky chops? Were you asleep, my little treasure?' Kylie crooned. 'Yes, bacon would wake anybody up, wouldn't it? We can all see you're starved,' she jested, rubbing Hayley's hairy belly. 'Now I am going to have to wash my hands. We will play later, missy.'

As the sun rose, a beautiful rainbow crystal positioned on the window ledge reflected onto the kitchen's oak walls. Taylor noted the image, tracing it back to its source. Kylie's unit contained very feminine pastel colours compared to his sparse military barracks smelling of floor polish, men and sweat. Floral arrangements adorned the lounge coffee table and the kitchen table. With breakfast almost cooked, Kylie began clearing her kitchen table of the array of nursing texts, building plans and books on crystals, angels and animal spirit guides. The variety suggested to Taylor that the nurse pivoted on a pendulum between fact and fantasy.

'How can I help?' Taylor offered, taking in Kylie's cute little button nose covered with a fine smattering of freckles. Her symmetrical facial features seemed perfectly aligned to her heart-shaped face.

'You can tell me how you have your tea or coffee. Or would you prefer a juice?'

'Coffee, white and one, would be grand, thanks.'

Taylor smiled, taking both their drinks to the dinner

table. Kylie's weak black coffee was poured into a jade-coloured angel cup with an inscription wishing that everyone had an angel by their side. Taylor held the plates closer for Kylie to land the bacon.

'How do you like your eggs cooked?'

'Both sides, thanks.'

Kylie smiled radiantly at that. Her dad used to tell her when she was a teenager, 'If a young man asks you how you have your eggs in the morning, always say, "Unfertilised, thank you".' Kylie shook her head, wondering where that lust-filled thought had come from. Not missing her amused grin, Taylor found he was fascinated by her soft, full, rosy lips and dimpled cheeks. He struggled to get the sensation of holding her captive in his chest and arms out of his thoughts. His first impression of her tiny shoulders had been the sensation of holding a child, when the pocket rocket suddenly turned, slamming into his thorax. At the memory of holding Kylie, Taylor's body began physically responding. To hide his dilemma, Taylor scooped down to pat and pick up the loyal pet who had been wagging her tail excitedly and licking his toes to get attention. Hayley began shaking a tiny floppy teddy bear in her teeth to initiate a tug of war game.

'You are a little cutie, aren't you?'

Mhhh, you both are, Taylor thought, bemused.

Immediately after her pick-up, Hayley began moving her legs and squirming frantically, wanting to hop down again. When her enthusiastic little paws made contact with the floor, Hayley dashed off to get a tiny silicone ball. As Taylor rolled it along the corridor, Hayley pranced to fetch it, keen to keep their game happening.

'Pets are one of the few things I miss from civilian life.'

'Yes, they are very therapeutic. They welcome you when you come home and are always unconditionally happy to see you. Hayley is my source of endless joy. I would need to take her to Jack's with me too, of course.'

'That would be fine. Dad loves animals. Hayley will amuse him too. She is very affectionate.'

'She's adorable.'

After setting down their plates with bacon rashers, eggs, fried tomato and toast, Kylie added a tiny saucer with chopped up bacon next to the water bowl beside the fridge.

'Let me repay your hospitality by taking you out for a meal tonight,' Taylor suggested.

'Thank you. That would be lovely. It's not necessary, though.'

'I insist. Can we go back to the hospital after a nap to check on Dad's progress? You will have to tell me where you'd like to dine, too, so I can book the restaurant.'

'Sure. How about you come back here tonight again? I can drop you at Jack's on Friday or Saturday to look around after we get whatever groceries you need.'

'That would be great. Do you have today off?'

'Yes, I asked my boss to give me a rostered day off so I could sit with Jack when he was unstable last night.'

'Thanks for that. I really appreciate your kindness to Dad and me. My defence force job now has me travelling further and more often than I would like. It has been full on at work ... I was feeling truly maxed out. I will stay with Dad tomorrow at the hospital, then get his car fuelled up and stock up on groceries on Saturday, if that suits?'

'Well, after we wake up, we can visit Jack tonight before dinner. I'm working Friday and Saturday, so I will just briefly check up on Jack on those afternoons. I hope I can spend more time with him Sunday. How about I drop you at the hospital tomorrow morning and pick you up about 4 pm?'

'I really appreciate everything you've done for us. To be honest, I am finding Dad's situation overwhelming. Seeing Dad like that was more gruelling than the last six months of unpredictable military life. I feel so drained at the moment.' Taylor hung his head. 'I am so ashamed of how I reacted to this crisis. When I heard you saying something, I jumped to wrong conclusions in my panic. I am not usually this reactive. I am generally more controlled rather than this emotionally labile.'

Kylie looked up after detecting his quivering voice. She caught a brief glimpse of Taylor's anguished, tear-filled eyes before he covered his face. Kylie bent towards him, placing a sympathetic arm on his shoulders.

'You are welcome to stay here as long as you need, Taylor. The best way to manage a crisis is to take things one day at a time. I will help you through this challenge. Just let me know what you need. Unfortunately, if Jack's car won't start, I will need my car for work on Friday, Saturday and during the week. You know, Sunday may be better to get Jack's car going. You're dealing with enough upheaval right now. It's more crucial for you to just focus on spending time with Jack while his condition is so critical.'

'Seeing Dad like that made me feel gutted. Utterly helpless! It's like there are all these machines around Dad supporting him, but the outcome relies on his determination to live. I'm sorry that I couldn't discuss that resuscitation plan with the doctor either. It was too much all at once.'

Taylor wiped away the tears spilling over his eyelids.

'Dr O'Brien was happy just to update you and leave the critical decisions for later. Sometimes, these situations determine themselves. Factors like age and frailness can sometimes take those decisions out of everyone's hands.'

'The only instruction I could give was to tell him to do the best for my dad. I don't want Dad to suffer if there is no benefit or chance for a good outcome.'

'They understood what you meant, Taylor. The doctors and nurses will give Jack the best possible chance to get through this. Originally, the questions were about Dr O'Brien and the medical team trying to determine Jack's pre-admission functional status. Dr O'Brien was also hinting that at seventy-two years of age, Jack may not have the physiological reserve to cope with pain, strenuous physiotherapy or the demands of a severe illness. He was being reserved about the outcome. To be brutally honest, Taylor, I feel like you do. If they cannot make Jack well enough to enjoy a good quality of life, I would prefer he did not suffer. I'd prefer Jack to be kept comfortable than be subjected to heroic measures.'

'Thank you. Your experience in the health field helps me to simplify and clarify things rather than being emotional. I hope you can be there when any crucial decisions need to be made. I want Dad given the best possible chance to survive.'

'After brekky, if you like, I'll give you my phone number. That way, you can ring me and put me on speaker for any medical discussions if you are unsure.'

'Yes, we'll do that. I'd be grateful for any advice.'

'Sometimes, the choices for resuscitation plans don't need to be just black and white, like whether to resuscitate or not. You can tell the doctors that you don't want some resuscitation measures that could cause pain like cardiac compressions, or defibrillation where they deliver electrical shocks to start the heart. You can ask the team to administer intravenous medications, a choice called a chemical resuscitation. If Jack's heart goes too slow, for example, they can give drugs to increase the rate. Choosing chemical resuscitation is like choosing the middle ground. It avoids painful and not necessarily beneficial measures.'

Taylor sighed deeply. 'I will certainly value your opinion when those decisions need to be made, Kylie. You know Dad fairly well too, it seems. He wanted quality, not quantity, of life.'

'Do you mind if I ask whether Jack has any other family, like brothers, sisters, nephews and nieces you should be informing? Would he like a minister of religion for prayers?'

'Oh,' Taylor gasped. 'I should let my cousin know. Jack's siblings have died, but my cousin might want to visit Dad. He stayed with him when he went to university here. That's a good idea about a minister too.'

'Let's write ourselves a note for when we wake up.'

'I'm glad Dad had a lovely nurse such as you caring for him,' Taylor said, tearing up again.

'I hope Jack can recover, so that together we can accommodate his wish.'

'Me too.'

Taylor reached over to hold Kylie's tiny hand, giving it a squeeze. To his surprise, the nurse had rough, scarred, hardworking hands, not at all what he'd anticipated. They felt like coarse sandpaper. After they placed their dishes in the sink to wash later, Taylor turned to give Kylie a brief thank you hug. With Kylie only 163 cm tall and feeling her warm breath at his sternum, his chin settled down on her head. To Taylor's horror, his body chemistry responded to the warm embrace, and he released her instantly. Taylor wanted to ask her so many personal questions, but now was not the time. His emotions were in enough turmoil without an unexpected physical attraction. Oblivious, Kylie left to take a shower.

Taylor slept restlessly. His nightmare of seeing his father attached to a ventilator was mingled with confusing, intrusive dreams of Kylie. In his dreams, Kylie was living at his father's house. Taylor awoke startled after dreaming they were sharing his bed. He drifted off again only to dream he was excited to be returning home to them both. In his dreams, Kylie had welcomed him with the same white-teethed, dimpled smile but the warm hug became more passionate. The dream became erotic when Kylie had surrendered to his needs in his childhood bed. Taylor woke up tenting the sheets.

Before leaving his room, Taylor modestly covered himself in a shave coat. He found Kylie sitting at the kitchen table, staring intently at a sandalwood scented candle with a clock in front of her. Kylie was wearing white cotton pyjama shorts and a top with pink and red tiny roses scattered over them. With her head bent intently forward, a small amount of cleavage was visible. Kylie's shoulders were tanned and bare except for the two tiny pink satin straps complementing the floral design. Kylie's sandy brown, long, wavy hair was tussled and loose. The effect was breathtaking, not helping his morning wood at all. Taylor was glad his shave coat was concealing the mesmerising effect, as Kylie looked up from the flame, with bright blue eyes.

'I'm just clearing my head,' she explained. With her make-up removed, her soft facial features, with the smattering of freckles on her nose, were naturally pretty.

'How does that work?'

'You stare at the flame for five minutes, acknowledging and releasing any random thoughts that come to mind. The goal is to focus on the shimmering flame to empty your mind of non-stop thoughts.'

'That's a handy trick,' Taylor smiled.

The kitchen rainbow had changed to a different position with the sun's movement across the sky, making the seven colours more vivid and vibrant.

'Come and try,' offered Kylie, a smile tugging at the corners of her lips.

'I might make my bladder gladder first, after all that coffee.'

'You can do the same exercise, using the red "power off lights" on equipment,' Kylie suggested when he returned. 'It is about quietening an overactive mind.'

With his head supported by both hands, Taylor stared at the flickering blue flame, watching the tip of the flame fluctuate with yellow, orange and red flickering movements. His mind flooded with thoughts, like worrying about his dad and needing to ring his cousin and the minister. As he dismissed the thoughts, Taylor became more peaceful. He found himself inhaling deeply and becoming more relaxed. Kylie sat there longer. Taylor looked up to find her staring intently at his face.

'Do you feel calmer now?'

'Yes. It took me a bit of effort to get on top of the dramas flushing through my brain. But when I did, the effect was soothing.'

Taylor looked at Kylie's small bracelet, as he contemplated how her philosophy of life infused into her living space. The rainbow, the crystals and angel books – all suited the mood of the room.

Kylie followed his gaze, idly touching the crystals. 'This bracelet is made of rose quartz and clear crystals.'

'You're into alternative therapies, then?'

'Yes. I find crystals fascinating. Since they contain silicon dioxide and oxygen, they can be compressed or expanded at different vibrational energies for healing. A NASA space physicist studied the amazing ability of crystals to transform, transmit, amplify and store light and sound energy.'

'You seem to like science, Kylie,' Taylor said, tentatively touching the elegant little bracelet.

'Yes, I truly do. I studied alternative medicine as part of my Bachelor of Health Science. I was fascinated by how crystals can influence the human life force energy through the seven chakras or energy vortexes distributed along the middle of the human body. I use these crystals to boost my energy.'

'They seem very delicate and shaped.'

'Yes, they are. As an energy form, the crystals are finicky about how they can be charged and cleaned in other energy mediums like sunlight. They need to be stored in sunlight, silk or cotton fabrics to maintain their integrity. If the crystal is not cut symmetrically or imperfectly so chips develop, it can reduce the energy level.'

'I like the pretty pink love hearts.'

'Me too. The clear quartz crystal works on the crown chakra at the crown of the head, and the rose quartz works on the throat and heart chakras to balance energy fields and release emotional blockages like grief,' Kylie explained. 'The crystals can influence the energy of the people around you. That was one of the reasons why I was holding Jack's hand. I wanted to let Jack know he was not alone, and I was also trying to give his life force an energy boost. Spiritualists believe people have layers like onions. Patients admitted to the Intensive Care Unit, like Jack, have their life force energy depleted down to their survival core energy.'

'Well, it's 3 pm. Would you like to go to the hospital now and recharge Dad?' Taylor smiled cheekily, lightening the moment.

'Yes,' Kylie replied, elbowing him in retaliation. 'We can leave a clear crystal in his shirt pocket and replace it every day. There is no harm done by supplementing traditional and complementary medicine, provided we notify the staff the crystal is there. Those testing human energy transfers believe that one hand (often the non-dominant hand) receives energy from the divine power source, and the other hand, usually the dominant hand, can deliver energy for healing.'

'Lordie! Well, don't touch Dad with the wrong hand. He can't afford to get his battery drained,' Taylor teased. 'I can't wait to see how Dad is today! I rang him every week when I could, until the last mission went on radio silence. I hope Dad remembered that. I hope he did not forget or think I was abandoning him.'

'Jack did not feel abandoned. He knew I was trying to contact you. He spoke fondly about how much he loved "his boy". Although Jack did not understand why we could not contact you, he just said, "My boy must be busy." Rest assured, Jack felt very loved. "He'll ring when he can," Jack confidently reassured me. Jack was very proud to be your father and Michelle's husband. In fact, he considered his greatest achievements in life were making you both happy. So, it made sense to me when you said the messages were not passed on.'

'Messages are usually posted into mailbox slits in our lockers. Mine will still be there. I have not been near my locker for the last six months since I was posted overseas. When the urgent hospital message came, I was immediately put onto flights to come directly here. The army only relay urgent messages like Dad's ICU admission through the official channels using our identity number rather than our name.'

'Is it better to communicate through email then?'

'Maybe. It depends on the nature and location of the mission.'

When they arrived in ICU, Jack was still ventilated but stable. The doctor had intentionally lightened Jack's sedation for a neurological assessment. The doctor planned to keep Jack stable for another day before trying to wean him from the ventilator. While they both sat there, Jack opened his eyes and looked at them both. With the breathing tube in his throat separating his vocal cords, Jack could not talk. When he tried to, Jack began coughing, then gagging, on the tube. Jack responded appropriately to commands. He squeezed hands as instructed and lifted his legs. Taylor and Kylie told Jack the day, date and time. They alerted Jack that he had fractured his skull when he climbed under his neighbour's house. Sweating profusely after his coughing fit, Jack nodded and squeezed both of their hands again. Jack raised his right arm, holding Taylor's hand, to his forehead and frowned. He nodded to questions, confirming he had a headache.

Intravenous paracetamol was added to the narcotic infusion being administered to provide greater comfort. With one of them on either side of the bed holding a hand, there was less risk of Jack trying to pull the breathing tube out.

'Dad, I am so sorry that I did not get the messages,' Taylor desperately reiterated. 'I was overseas on a mission. I only got flown back last night. When you get better, we are going to try to keep you at home, Dad. If you can pass all the medical tests, we have found a solution that is safe for you to stay home. Don't worry, Dad.'

Speechless, Jack's eyes remained focused on his son.

'You can't talk with that tube in. You are doing well. Just get better for us,' Taylor pleaded. 'I'm on leave for a month now, so we will have plenty of time together. I need your best effort! I will come and see you every day. I love you, Dad!'

Jack squeezed both hands in approval. His sedation was increased when he began to tire.

Kylie and Taylor left the hospital around 7 pm.

'That was pleasing to see,' Kylie confirmed.

'You think so?'

'Yes. Jack was responding as though he recognised us. He reacted appropriately to commands like squeezing our hands. Jack will fatigue easily. To me, Jack was communicating a headache. He nodded at your voice. There are no guarantees that Jack will do well, but I believe he was found early enough to be able to make the most of this chance.'

'I pray that thought travels from your lips to God's ears, Kylie.'

'Jack even winked at me in the cheeky way he usually does.'

'Yes, I saw that.'

'Jack usually winks at me like that when he is trying to get away with something mischievous. Jack winks when he slips a chocolate bar or marshmallows in with his groceries. He winked right after we mentioned about his hiding under the neighbour's house. Jack seemed very alert today. On his birthday, Jack winked before detouring from the grocery shop to the baker's to buy a small caramel or lemon delicious tart.'

Taylor laughed. 'That sounds like my old man. He's always been a sweet tooth. Mum used to make sure we each had a party every year for our birthdays. Dad could never hold back with the caramel tarts or lollies.'

'When we unpack his groceries, Jack usually put his treats in the top kitchen drawer near the fridge. Then he points playfully saying, "Now don't you tell the doc".'

'As a child, Dad always told me not to tell Mum. It was hilarious when I actually caught Mum stocking up his treats. Mum kept a few small chocolate bars in the pantry. When Dad's drawer supply was diminishing, Mum and I would take one from the bottom shelf of the pantry to stock his rations up. If Dad ever noticed, he never said.'

'That's funny. I used to hide a chocolate bar in the bottom drawer of my dressing kit, too! I'd stock him up on Tuesdays and Wednesdays, before the grocery shop on Thursdays, to prevent him wandering off. I snuck it in there after his shower while he was sitting in front of the mirror shaving,' Kylie confessed, laughing. 'No wonder he's a sugar junkie.'

'Dad would get in trouble from Mum if we had a chocolate bar before our evening meal. We could share a chocolate after tea before we cleaned our teeth for bed, but not before our evening meal. If Dad got caught breaking off half the squares for me earlier, he was in trouble for setting a bad example. One day, Mum made us laugh. She said, "It's very quiet in here. I hope my boys aren't eating chocolate." We both giggled so much we had brown chocolate saliva running down our chins. We were sprung badly. It was hilarious.'

'I am going to buy Jack a box of caramel chocolates for his first flavour to taste when he gets off that machine! The 8 or 9 mm tube in his throat has to be big enough to deliver a sizable breath within a limited time frame, and sometimes, ventilated patients get a sore throat from that wide bore breathing tube. So, let's get Jack a reward for his achievement.'

Taylor nodded in agreement.

'He really enjoyed one particular Australian brand that I bought for his birthday. The whole box was gone in two days. Jack just loved them! Although truth be known, sugar in any form might be a hit.'

Taylor smiled, still indulging his childhood memories. 'Yes, we will get them tonight and take them up tomorrow. That will spur him on. Not that anyone could go wrong with Dad and chocolate.'

Chapter Six

Sally's magnetism

*G*reg was entranced, watching Sally's expressive eyes and animated facial expressions as they washed Joe's faecally stained limbs. Sally frowned and creased her eyes, wincing at the smell as she tried not to retch. Wearing face masks sprayed on the outside with Sally's perfume, both nurses only exposed and lifted a single limb at a time.

'I bet you a canteen coffee after we finish work today that we will have Joe's core temperature at 34 degrees before we go home.'

'I'll say 33 degrees. And make it a chamomile tea for me if I win. I won't sleep if I have coffee before bedtime.'

'Deal.'

'How come you don't go to any of the staff parties, Sally?'

'It's kind of ... well ... we are around people all the time in this profession, aren't we? It really makes me value my quiet time.'

'To do what?'

'Oh, catch up on housework, gardening, watch movies, read, pay bills, do crafts – whatever. Just "me" time, when I only have to please myself, not others.'

'Got anything special planned for your days off?'

'After I get home, I usually sleep until midday. Then I try to stay awake until 7 pm to get back into a normal sleeping pattern. I just laze around on my first day off. I am usually too fatigued to work or study. Sometimes, I just go to the beach or for walks for exercise to be self-disciplined; otherwise, I might be tempted to sleep my days off away. With my science exams around the corner, I suppose I should put in more effort, though.'

'There's a scientific conference next month for the ICU network in Sydney. Are you going?'

'Yes, I like to stay up to date with the current research and evidence-based practice recommendations. With a mortgage, I can't afford holidays, so I requested four days off in addition to the two study days we are entitled to as a reward for sitting my exams.'

'I'm going too, I haven't booked anything yet. Where are you staying?'

'At the motel beside the conference centre. I forget its name. I chose that accommodation to save money on taxis. On the map, that motel is close to a huge shopping mall in the same street.'

'That's a great idea.'

The next time Greg walked to the desk to answer the phone, he collected the roster folder to ask for additional days off. Greg brought the roster and study leave forms back to complete at Joe's bedside. He wanted to use his study leave to attend the conference as well as ask for the same four days off requested in red by Sally. Everyone was able to choose five special requests in red each month's roster. Greg was desperately hoping that spending social time at the conference together might move him out of the "friend zone".

At 7 am, Joe's monitor temperature recording was 33.5 degrees. Not wanting to relinquish the opportunity, Greg brought Sally her tea. Both nurses' faces had matching indentations on their noses from wearing the perfume-sprayed masks all night to escape the foul faecal stench. Even the vanilla fragrance exuded from the deodorising machine they'd borrowed from the mortuary had failed to overcome Joe's extremely pungent odour.

'Oh, this chamomile tea tastes great. Thanks, Greg.'

'It's definitely my pleasure! Thank you for helping me to scrub both Jack and Joe back into human form. I could not believe my "luck" of having ants and maggots two nights in a row.'

'At least a busy night makes the time go faster.'

'Yes, it feels better than struggling to stay awake at a dimly lit, quiet bed area.'

'Absolutely.'

Since the conference advertised several free breakfast events catered by a pharmacy company promoting drug products and an expensive gala event, all needing to be pre-booked, Greg opened his conference book to discuss their schedule with Sally. With Sally routinely attending the ICU scientific conference every year, she had favourite speakers whose presentations she regularly attended. Greg circled those sessions to make them a priority.

'This intensivist is a researcher with his own publishing company,' Sally indicated, pointing to a name Greg did not recognise. 'His talks on his Belgium research of the lung alveoli, sepsis and immune responses are usually stimulating and well-illustrated.'

Greg turned the page over to the social page in the middle of the brochure. 'Would you like to share accommodation to make it cheaper?' Greg asked, intentionally not looking up from the page immediately in case his enthusiasm was apparent. 'Have you booked or paid for anything yet?'

Looking at the booklet upside down, Sally searched for the venue she recognised next door to the conference centre. Greg used the opportunity to move his chair closer.

'This is where I had planned on staying for five nights and six days,' clarified Sally, looking for a two-bedroom suite. 'We could try to book this family room. You're right. It would be cheaper than two separate bookings.'

'I could ring the conference coordinators and arrange that, if you're happy? Would you let me pay for the

Saturday night gala too? I would like to take you there.'

'Are you sure? It's quite expensive, especially when you need to pay for evening wear as well.'

'Yes, absolutely! There is a brilliant band playing. It should be loads of fun. As you said, it is right across the road from our accommodation, so we will save on taxis.'

Wanting to repay Greg's generosity, Sally came up with a solution. 'Okay, well, if you're shouting the gala dinner, I will pay for us to visit the zoo.' Studying the schedule, Sally searched for the day where the afternoon lunch presentations looked less inviting. 'This Friday, I was just going to attend the morning presentations. I could not find anything I was particularly interested in at the afternoon sessions, which seem to be dedicated to allied health workers like the dieticians. They are all about nutrition, calorie research and physio techniques. For our two days' paid study leave, we only need to spend sixteen hours at the conference. What do you think?'

'That sounds good.'

Greg bit his lip, keen to disguise his sheer delight at the opportunity of spending so much time with Sally. Now that Sally had agreed to attend the gala dinner, he was looking forward to dancing and having a few drinks with her. He flattened his hands on his knees to mask his enthusiasm.

'The ferries leave regularly from Circular Quay to Taronga Zoo, or we could take a water taxi across the harbour if we miss one.'

'What about flights?'

'I booked to arrive Monday morning at 10 am and leave the Sunday afternoon on the 4.45 pm flight,' clarified Sally.

'Well, I will try to book the same flights so we can travel together to reduce taxi fares. I can pick you up and we can leave my car in the long-term parking at the airport. Do I need to talk to Tina about the rosters first?'

'Yes, that would be a good idea. I marked my requests in red, but it is better to confirm the roster before paying for any bookings.'

'Okay, then. You confirm the accommodation bookings, and I will confirm the flight bookings when the roster is published tomorrow, yeah?'

Sally nodded.

As they both headed home to sleep off their night shifts, Greg recorded in his diary a reminder to hire or buy a suit on the Saturday morning. When his brain was foggy from circadian disruption, Greg had learnt to function by writing every idea down as he thought of them. Usually when working the night shifts, Greg was so fatigued during the day that he felt blessed just to generate a thought. Rather than rely on keeping his plans in his head, Greg made lists. The lists gave him direction about what urgent things needed to be covered on his days off.

Chapter Seven
The tradie ladies

*S*aturday morning, Greg was absolutely shocked. As he navigated a barricade, making his way to the menswear shops at the mall to sort out his suit for the gala dinner, he heard the loud crack of a staple gun in a new store being renovated. *Ca-chung, ca-chung*, the staple gun sounded as the staples embedded into timber. Greg abruptly stopped in his tracks when he recognised Sally, her knees locked standing on a ladder, in high visibility navy and yellow work clothes. Sally's concentration was focused as she stapled in the ceiling cornice. She was wearing clear eye protection and had yellow ear plugs in. As Greg went to sit on a bench to watch this unexpected spectacle, he was surprised to find Jack's son, Taylor, there, already seated.

'Hey, mate,' greeted Taylor with a solid handshake.

'How are you going?' Greg asked, returning the greeting.

'Yeah, not too bad, mate,' Taylor conceded. 'Dad is

coming off the breathing machine this morning. The nurses told me to come back after 11 am, so I decided to come shopping to grab a few supplies. When I heard the renovation noise, I looked over and was surprised to see Kylie working in there.'

'I met Kylie the night Jack was admitted. She stayed in ICU helping us wash him. I hadn't recognised her. I am surprised to see Sally up there wielding a staple gun.'

'Why would these girls be working two jobs?' Taylor enquired, wearing a puzzled expression. At around 163 cm, he had always considered Kylie to be short until she stood beside Sally, who was only around 157 cm in height.

'I'm not sure. The night your dad was admitted, I realised that Sally and Kylie knew each other well. I got the impression they go to uni together. Neither had mentioned they both work a second job together.'

'For qualified skilled nurses, they both look efficient and competent in this trade as well. Actually, sitting here watching them both, I get the impression they both work regularly in the building industry together.'

'They do, don't they!'

Both men sat silent admiring the measured confident movements of the tradie ladies. Greg could not divert his eyes away from Sally's trim toned butt. His eyes wandered down to her steel capped shoes but were diverted by watching Kylie measuring and marking out the benchtops ready for installing.

No wonder power tools occupy so much space in the back

of her car, Taylor thought.

'When I stopped to watch Kylie, I expected to find they were working for a male builder. But it has just been these two tradie ladies here on their own,' Taylor elaborated, concerned the nurses were financially strained. 'They work in a very coordinated manner, as though they do building contracts together regularly. I've been watching them both for about an hour. They both know what they are doing. They check plans together and function like an established team with a long history.'

In the silence, Taylor's mind recalled the plans that Kylie had hastily relocated from her dining room table.

Greg said, 'Most nurses come out of uni with at least a $30,000 higher education debt, just for their bachelor degree. Of course, that loan probably doubles for those doing their master's, as Sally is.'

'I suppose they would be paying rent or rates too.'

'Most nurses usually have private health cover, too. The public hospital waiting list is controlled by time, so it features long waiting lists. In contrast, the private sector is controlled by what the market will bear, so most nurses get private insurance cover as pay deductions when their employers offer great corporate deals. I suppose they could be paying car payments too. Reliable vehicles are usually a priority for shift-working females. I know Sally "salary packaged" a car recently after her old vehicle kept breaking down.'

'But what would they be spending all their money on

to need to work two jobs?'

'Well, I can tell you it is not drugs or alcohol. They are both as sharp as tacks. I'd say it's just living expenses.'

Greg couldn't help but notice Taylor watching Kylie's every move.

Greg said, 'Sally told me that Kylie lives very modestly in a two-bedroom unit. If these girls are licensed builders, I imagine they could also be paying double registration and union fees in the nursing and builders associations?'

'Yes, I suppose they would have to. I still wonder why they are both so broke they need to work two jobs.'

'I didn't realise that when Sally mentioned her mother needed a new bathroom, to remove a bathtub after her knee replacement, that she was planning on doing it all herself. Both must be financially strained, perhaps.'

'Yes. I'm wondering whether they are financially strained themselves or helping out poorer family members.' Looking towards Greg, Taylor asked, 'Are you as astonished as I am?'

'Well, I suppose we both knew these girls were intelligent and capable.'

'Very capable!' Taylor conceded.

'Honest, too,' commented Greg, thinking about ICU's single mother, Alice, stealing toilet paper and tissues.

'I am absolutely gobsmacked, sitting here watching this pair. I can't work half the tools that I've watched them use expertly this morning.'

'Me, neither. Sally has dug me out of a few conundrums

at work, let me tell you! One time, in dim night lighting, there was so much blood and oral secretions around a ventilated multi-trauma's face that I accidently cut the balloon inflation port off a patient's breathing tube. At the time, I was trying to change the bloodstained ties securing the breathing tube. Sally efficiently increased the oxygen supply on the ventilator to one hundred per cent, then instructed me to suction the saliva pooling at the back of the patient's mouth to prevent aspiration into his lungs. Almost paralysed by fear at my own stupidity, I watched Sally skilfully thread the plastic insert of an intravenous cannula down the severed plastic pilot tube of the breathing tube. I was awestruck, watching Sally proceed to reinflate the cuff with a syringe. Instead of having an airway emergency to replace the breath tube urgently, Sally had rescued me.'

'Yes, they are both competent. I am rather concerned they need to work two jobs just to make ends meet financially, though.'

'Maybe it is to buy extra things. I know that Sally goes to the ICU scientific conferences every year to combine education with a four-day, tax-deductible holiday. Sally takes extra days off so she can afford a four-day holiday by claiming the flights and accommodation on tax. From what I'm seeing, it seems likely they spend their other holidays and days off building.'

'That is appalling, though, don't you think?'

'I do. But I am not sure that either of us will be able to help these girls. We cannot critically judge them for getting their income honestly through hard work, can we?'

'You know,' Taylor continued, 'I was wondering who fixed Dad's weathered back doorway. I was going to fix it on my next visit home. The doorway was such an odd size that I had to order an external door to be made. The manufactured door had not arrived before I left, so I was intending to install it on my next visit home. This morning, when I used Dad's keys to get inside, I found it was already repaired. Let me tell you, the professional work done squaring up that doorway was amazing. I was left in no doubt that work was done by an experienced builder. It was a better job than I could ever have done. Dad's jamming bedroom window was fixed too. There were homemade meals in the fridge like cottage pie, spaghetti bolognaise and tuna mornay, all labelled and dated. Now I think I know who has done all this, I am wondering how I can repay my gratitude.'

'They work hard in nursing, too. I wonder how long they have sustained working two jobs.'

'I think you and I both need to tread carefully,' Taylor suggested.

'How do you mean?'

'Well, you seem to me to be as interested in Sally as I am in Kylie. We need to proceed carefully to see how we can support these hardworking tradie ladies. If they get suspicious, we could injure their pride and get the bum's rush.'

'So, you are dating Kylie, then?'

'I wish! No, this is the first time we've ever met. Dad's last nurse left on five years of maternity leave. I stupidly jumped to ridiculous conclusions on my first introduction to Kylie, so we got off to a bumpy start. What about you?'

'I have been hinting to Sally that I'd like to date her. Sally is my team leader, so I have to be careful not to let my personal life encroach on my work life. To be honest, Sally is so intelligent, experienced and capable that I constantly feel outclassed.'

'Yes, watching this, I'd say we both probably are. I know just how you feel. Do you think these tradie ladies are so bloody capable that they demasculinise us?'

'Probably,' Greg laughed. 'Sally is all business at work. Seeing this now, I understand why she has no desire for a social life. Sally and I are attending a work conference together in Sydney next month, so I am trying to work up the courage to ask her to date me then. At the same time, if she's not agreeable, I have to be careful not to ruin the only holiday Sally takes off in a year. Perhaps I should ask her during our flight home.'

'I'm only on family leave for a month while Dad's recovering, so my time and opportunities with Kylie will be limited, too. I see now that I will have less time than I imagined, since she works five days a week and has a second job. Kylie had seemed oddly evasive about what she was doing today. She drove to the hospital at 7 am to visit Dad with me and left me there for the day. I wonder whether she went home again to change into her tradie clothes or if she keeps a spare set in her car. Now that I think about it, if their second job is supposed to be a secret, they might not appreciate catching us sitting here watching them.'

'I could watch Sally all day,' Greg sighed, stretching out his long legs to cross them at his ankles.

'Man, you've got it bad, too,' Taylor insisted, staring with rapt attention at the skilled tradie ladies.

'You're telling me nothing new!' laughed Greg. 'It's pretty hard to make a move to date a female boss. I have been trying to strategically find ways to spend extra time with her. Every event I have invited Sally to has been tactfully declined. Now that I see she is working two jobs, I can understand why Sally is not keen to socialise.'

'Watching these competent tradie ladies at work distorts the whole helpless feminine images we've been socialised into.'

'Yes, our relationships with these women will definitely be egalitarian.'

'While I am confident we have both been taught to respect women, I understand what you mean. I feel profoundly outclassed too. If we are successful, it will most likely be because we are playing to our strengths, like using our charm and humour!'

'Yes, they both need lightening up. They tend to be fairly serious, and infinitely kind.'

'So, we could help them relax and have fun.'

'I think I'd better leave before I get sprung,' declared Greg. 'Good luck, mate.'

'You, too,' Taylor said, shaking Greg's hand. 'Just remember, these two may be strong independent women, but they are vulnerable too. Our role could be to support them to reach their objectives. Interdependence, not independence, is the mature state. We can make these women happy by providing them with supportive stable relationships – if they allow us.'

'Well, I will be giving Sally my maximum effort.'

'Kylie deserves mine, too. I think it is important that we find our place in the relationships we want to build with them.'

'Hmmm, I like a challenge.'

'It will be worth it. I guess them being so different to any other girls we have ever dated could be part of our attraction to them.'

'Good to chat, mate. I better go. I am off to buy a suit.' With a final handshake, the men separated.

Taylor sat down again to continue observing the tradie ladies. However, like Greg, Taylor began to feel uncomfortable. Watching these ladies, who seemed to have gone to extremes to keep their second job private, made him feel like a stalker. Taylor checked his watch before heading back to his father's hospital bed.

Perturbed and still trying to integrate this new information, he hesitantly took another look before leaving. Unhappy and concerned, Taylor stopped in his tracks, indulging himself with a final look to commit to memory. His eyes fixated on the image of Kylie in her trim work wear. He replayed in his head how Kylie had evasively mentioned having commitments this morning. Kylie had offered to pick him up at 4 pm to check on Jack's progress. Remaining bewildered, Taylor looked over again at Kylie sawing off the cornice at what appears to be a 45-degree angle to pass up to Sally. Learning this new information made him feel like the biggest bastard ever.

Chapter Eight
Young's syndrome

*A*s he walked past the nurses' station on his return to ICU, Taylor overheard Dr O'Brien on the phone requesting a respiratory physician to review his father's chronic lung disease.

There was nothing new about his father's rattly chest and hacking cough. Those noises had always been a normal part of their lives, as his father's respiratory symptoms had persisted for years. Taylor had known all about his father's damaged airways, always referred to as bronchiectasis, and his inflamed sinuses, since he was often prescribed long-term antibiotics. What was odd was that Dr O'Brien had informed the other consultant that his father had Young's syndrome. Getting out his phone, Taylor automatically researched the odd term, confident it was a respiratory condition. Taylor's intention was simply to become more familiar with the medical jargon in case it became relevant in the updates about his father's condition. The internet stated that Young's syndrome had predominantly three symptoms: bronchiectasis, chronic sinusitis – and infertility.

With a few overheard words, Taylor's world was suddenly turned upside down.

Taylor sat there stunned, staring at the word "infertility". Taylor had recalled from his science classes in school that there are only two major eye colours. Genetically, eyes are either blue or brown, with naturally brown eyes believed to be genetically dominant. (Green eyes were a yellow layer over blue eyes.) Some people with blue eyes carried both the brown and blue eye genes. His green eyes were explained as being the result of blue eye genes pairing. Since Jack and Michelle had brown eyes, Taylor had always assumed they both had the blue and brown eye genes, with the blue genes pairing.

Taylor's hands began to shake as he continued to read. He was shattered to learned that Young's syndrome occurred during childhood due to either mercury exposure or (as in Jack's case) an infection like the mumps. The internet described the infertility aspect of Young's syndrome as resulting from obstruction of the *vas deferens* tube in the epididymis of the male reproductive tract. If the sperm Jack's body produced became obstructed and unable to mix with the rest of his ejaculatory fluid in his epididymis tube, where sperm exited the testis, there was no way he could have fathered a child. The male infertility or "obstructive azoospermia" feature of the condition meant that the sperm of the male's semen was "non-existent". Jack could not be his father!

Still reeling from uncertainty, Taylor greeted his father with his usual affection. This new information did not change his strong feelings for the gentle man he had always assumed was his father. However, it raised many questions about his origins. Taylor became more convinced he was adopted. Were there other parents out there who had rejected him? Being currently in a hospital, Taylor even wondered if he could encounter inherited diseases he was oblivious of. The infertility news left Taylor feeling alienated, as though someone had stolen his identity. One family had raised him, making him feel so loved and doted on, but why had another relinquished him? What had happened to his birth parents? With his father's new diagnosis of dementia, would Jack be able to tell him the history behind his adoption? The accumulating effects of learning he was adopted, Jack's fragile condition and being surrounded by alarming machines caused Taylor to become tearful. The potential loss of losing the only father he had ever known was now amplified by feeling rejected by his birth parents.

You grow up assuming your parents are one of the few permanent features of your life, Taylor thought. *While most things change in your life, your parents are one of the assumptions you take for granted!*

Saddened immensely, Taylor began searching about

adoption. The research said that adopted children tend to retain the personalities of their biological parents. Jack was a quiet accountant; Taylor was a risk-taking special forces soldier. Unrestrained Taylor's feelings ran riot. Adoptees often have abandonment issues, affecting their ability to form relationships, he read, but Taylor had never felt abandoned. Jack and Michelle had loved him, and he had always felt welcome in their home. He had trusted his parents, having never experienced any reason not to. So, why was he now mentally thinking of his parents using their Christian names, instead of Mum and Dad?

Taylor's mind boggled with information overload and confusion. His escalating stress was generating thoughts that kept reverberating in revolving loops, causing exhaustion. When he read that adoptees tend to push people away and fail to form "attachments" in relationships, Taylor began analysing why he was still single at twenty-eight. Was his single status related to his career choice of travelling a lot with other male soldiers or was he subconsciously avoiding relationships? Holding Jack's warm hand, Taylor became increasingly unsettled. Were those biological stranger parents out there even looking for him? How did his adoption come about? *God,* Taylor thought, *why is all this doubt landing on me now!*

*

Jack opened his eyes and looked at Taylor, who was sitting with his head down, frantically tapping letters on the lit-up phone screen. After coming off the ventilator yesterday, Jack had never thought automated breathing could be such hard labour. While he hated the sensation of the nurses using a vacuum apparatus to remove his lung secretions, Jack had felt better afterwards. During the suctioning, Jack had learned to cough instantly, so the nurses did not push the vacuum tube down his airway so far as to trigger a cough. Now he felt too weak to cough up all that lung matter himself. As the ventilator support was reduced, and the breathing effort became under his control, Jack felt like he had a flat battery. It was like running a marathon – absolutely exhausting. When the doctor had ordered the external breathing machine to be strapped to his face, the burden was lifted.

Jack squeezed Taylor's hand, delighted to see his son again. Jack was intrigued at a fleeting expression that looked like guilt flash across Taylor's face.

'How are you, Dad?'

Taylor stood so that his father could see him better without twisting. Jack nodded.

'I bet it was good to get off that other machine, hey?'

'Bit tired,' gasped Jack, reserving his limited energy to breathe.

'I'm so glad to see you're getting better. You have been

making impressive progress every day.'

'Good to see you too, my boy,' Jack said breathlessly.

Taylor frowned at what his brain now perceived was a lie. Jack noticed the odd expression of doubt before closing his eyes in fatigue. Taylor forced a plastic smile that did not reach his eyes, before changing the subject.

'Do you remember what happened?' enquired Taylor.

'Not really.'

'Do you remember hiding under the neighbours' house, Dad?'

Jack's eyes opened and his eyeballs elevated to his right, trying to remember.

'I wanted to wait until you'd come home, son,' explained Jack.

'And you did, Dad,' Taylor smiled. 'Don't worry, we will sort this out.'

'Sometimes I'm getting forgetful,' Jack replied breathlessly.

'I have a month off now, Dad, so we will try to get you home again, if you are able.'

'Please.'

'The nurse had trouble contacting me, Dad. If they don't say matters are urgent when they ring, the messages just get dropped in my locker. I am so sorry, Dad.'

'Not your fault.'

'I will do everything I can to get you to stay at home, Dad. The nurse said there is a way someone can live in the house with you, and you can go into a day therapy centre for a few hours during the week.'

'Kylie ... kind ...' Jack whispered, smiling between laboured breaths. His voice was so weak Taylor had to move closer to hear.

'Yes, that would be a good choice, Dad. I met her last night.'

'Fixed door.'

'Yes, it is a good job, too. I got a taxi home this morning to check on everything while they took that tube out of your mouth. The nurses wanted you to have a natural sleep for two hours after your exertion.'

'I will get home,' Jack hoarsely whispered, but with determination.

'Good. I'd like that, Dad. I will check the car battery and fuel tomorrow.'

Jack looked puzzled, wondering how Taylor got to the hospital.

'Everything is fine, Dad. I just want to spend more time with you at the moment.'

'Window,' added Jack in a hoarse, weak whisper.

'Yes, she did a brilliant job fixing the jamming window, too!'

'Sometimes ... visits ... on weekends.' Jack smiled before adding, 'Did better job ... than I ... ever could!'

Laughing, Taylor's eyes lit up. 'Better than me as well.'

'Brings chocolates,' Jack smiled.

'You sound spoilt.'

'Spoilt is ... caramel tarts,' Jack whispered, tensing his

shoulder muscles to accommodate the effort.

He smiled weakly before dozing off again.

Taylor sat down again, studying his father's facial features. He took in the wrinkles that deepened and creased further at Jack's forehead and mouth. Jack's nose and chin had become more prominent with age. Jack's white hair was cut in his characteristic short back and sides style. He wonders how he could have been fooled into thinking Jack was his biological parent. It was like seeing a stranger for the first time. Instantly, Taylor became overwhelmed with grief. The nurse recording Jack's vital signs on the observation charts at the end of the bed walked over, offering social worker assistance. Taylor nodded, gratefully accepting the offer rather than contemplating his next move with uncertainty. Facts, like who his parents were, weren't facts anymore. The next moment, he felt totally selfish. While Jack struggled for every breath, he was tormented about his origins. Military life fostered ordered thinking, not this emotional maelstrom.

When the social worker, Annie, arrived, Taylor took the conversation outside. Annie, expecting to be discussing strategies to enhance Jack's ability to stay home, suddenly found the conversation taking an abrupt turn.

'How can I help?' Annie began.

'I have loads of questions,' Taylor replied. 'Some are about my dad and his ongoing care. But I am selfish, so some are about me.'

'About you?'

'Yes, about me. I have only recently discovered that Jack is not my biological father, as I had assumed my whole life.'

'Oh, so you did not know that you were adopted?'

'No!' Taylor angrily responded through clenched teeth. 'I most certainly did not!' Taylor's mind needed relief from the "what if" scenarios reverberating around in an endless loop of possibilities.

'So, would you like to find out about your biological parents?'

'I want to know everything. How this all came about? I understand about Dad's infertility issues, but why did my biological parents give me away? I need to know about their personal circumstances. How I can find out about them? I feel guilty asking about all this, because Jack and Michelle were the best parents ever. But suddenly, I feel like my whole life was a big conspiracy of silence, that people made decisions for me without my knowledge. Dad is sometimes forgetful, so while I am seriously concerned about his welfare, I also need to know who I am.'

'That is very reasonable, Taylor. That news came as a shock, by the sound of it.'

'Shock? I don't know who I am anymore! The people I assumed from birth were my parents seemed to have lied to me my whole bloody life!'

Chapter 9

Taylor's identity struggle

*J*ack was recovering amazingly well when Kylie caught up with him and Taylor at the hospital. The support delivered by the non-invasive ventilator was being weaned successfully. Kylie had imagined Taylor's mood would be more elevated now that Jack was able to communicate, yet Taylor looked in the gloomiest mood ever. Kylie believed he was masking his emotions at Jack's beside. His father was also puzzled by Taylor's blank canvas face devoid of emotions. For the whole visit, Jack looked so concerned that he did not shift his gaze from his son's face. After an hour of visiting, Taylor and Kylie left the hospital, heading out for their evening meal.

'Has something else happened?' Kylie questioned after they were seated in the restaurant. Taylor's face was etched in a constant frown.

After a pregnant pause ensued, Taylor challenged in

75

a confrontational manner, 'You tell me!'

Kylie looked up, surprised. Suddenly alert, Kylie was stunned to see hot salty tears spilling over Taylor's eyelids, a troubled, almost haunted expression across his face.

'What's happened?' Kylie leant forward, mystified.

'Are you part of all this grand conspiracy too?'

'Conspiracy? What is wrong?'

'Young's syndrome! Not bronchiectasis – Young's syndrome!' Taylor said, sculling down the entire pot of beer before signalling the waiter for another.

Kylie tried validating helpfully. 'Bronchiectasis is one of three symptoms of Young's syndrome.'

'Yes, exactly!' Taylor angrily tossed back his head, knocking back the second pot of beer. 'I know that. I bloody looked it up.'

'What am I missing?' Kylie gestured with her hands raised in the universal plea.

'What are the other symptoms?' challenged Taylor, angrily.

'The other two symptoms are sinusitis and azoospermia,' Kylie automatically responded.

'Exactly!' Taylor slammed the empty glass down, pointing to her animatedly before signalling for another beer.

Kylie was gobsmacked. 'You did not know?'

'No, I most certainly did not!' Taylor leant back, folding his arms across his impressively broad thorax. 'So, I repeat, are you part of this grand conspiracy?'

Cautiously picking her words due to Taylor's mercurial mood change, Kylie slowly replied, 'Until now, I had no idea that you did not know. Remember, this is the first time we have ever met.' Realising the massive impact this news had on Taylor, Kylie continued. 'I'm sorry that ... that ... you did not know.'

'What did Jack tell you?' Taylor demanded. Kylie intuitively noticed that Jack was no longer "Dad". Taylor was already distancing himself from the excruciating pain, the new knowledge conveyed.

'Jack has always told me that he loved you as much as Michelle. You both made his life whole. Jack always considered your happiness and Michelle's to be his greatest achievements. From what I surmised, if you had to be adopted, you could not have chosen better parents.'

'I am twenty-eight years old and suddenly finding out that I do not know who I am,' Taylor remarked angrily. He sculled his beer and ordered another.

'But you were told!' Kylie insisted. 'I remember now. Jack told me about it when he showed me a photo of you in your first Cubs uniform. He told me that photo was special. It had been taken just after they had summoned up the courage to tell you you were adopted. Jack had said that when he and Michelle had told you that you were "adopted", you went to school and had told your teacher they had said you were a doctor. Jack was amused because the teacher thought you were sick and had been taken to a doctor. The teacher had phoned Michelle concerned about your health. Jack said that he and Michelle had then had to clarify with you what "adopted" meant. Jack had said that you had taken the news in your stride. He had presumed that to be because your lives all went on as usual; nothing had changed. Michelle told you that "adopted" meant you were born from within her heart, not beneath it. I remember that, because I found her concept of adoption beautiful and loving. I got the impression that you were around five years old at the time, because "adopted" and "doctor" were new words in your vocabulary.'

'When did Dad say that?' Taylor questioned, keenly interested.

'The first time I heard the story behind the Cubs uniform photo was about five months ago, when I was using photos to assess Jack's memory. The photo story was brought up again only last week. Jack was selecting the photos in frames and albums he wanted to take to the nursing home. I think Jack would be horrified that you thought he was keeping a secret from you. I understood, from what Jack told me, that they had been instructed to tell you sooner rather than later. You probably felt so secure and loved that the news was not important at the time. Perhaps you did not really understand the implications of adoption due to your age. Humans tend to process information according to its relevance. Since as a five-year-old boy, your circumstances did not change, you probably had no reason to worry.'

'I honestly don't remember ever being told I was adopted. That news has been quite a shock. Mum had always told me my whole life that I grew in her heart. I remember there is a drawer at home of childhood drawings with love hearts and photos in them. There were childhood drawings where I had put her photo in a big love heart, too. Maybe that was what those drawings were all about. Maybe it was why Mum and Dad kept them.'

Taylor drank another pot.

'Do you think we should order a meal now?' Kylie asked timidly, alarmed at the amount of alcohol Taylor was consuming.

'Yes, of course,' Taylor replied apologetically, raking his hands over his face and through his thick short curls. 'I usually do not drink, but at the moment, I'm finding this is all too much.'

'How much would you usually drink?'

'I have probably had one beer in the last five years,' Taylor sighed, looking distraught.

'Well, let's order a meal. Then we can talk about how you feel and what you want to do about this new information. Talking and making decisions is usually more therapeutic than drowning your sorrows,' Kylie suggested in a soft caring tone. 'I can't imagine how distressed you felt, learning about your adoption accidentally. Your emotions were already fragile, with Jack being critically ill, without more traumatic information increasing your vulnerability.'

'I am finding all these challenges incredibly stressful. I worry that Jack might not pull through. I selfishly want information about how my adoption came about. I understand why Jack and Michelle adopted me, but why did my biological parents give me up? It felt like, in an instant, I did not know who I was anymore. It was like all the assumptions I had about my life were illusions.'

Kylie reached over the table to empathetically give Taylor's hand a gentle squeeze. Maintaining eye contact, Kylie attempted to soothe his distress in her soft voice.

'Taylor, I feel it is crucial that you still recognise yourself as the very loved son of Jack and Michelle Robinson. It is vital for you to remember that, as an important fact in all this uncertainty. Yes, you may have other brothers, sisters and parents in the world who I hope you can still connect with. I don't believe anyone intended to harm you.'

Kylie moved her chair closer to gently reassure him. Taylor hung his head, shamefully wiping a hand over his anguished face.

'I should be grateful to have had such amazing parents, shouldn't I?'

'Well, I think you always knew that you were loved. But the adoption news for you has raised other questions, about other biological family members you may want to connect with. Do you want to find out more about your biological parents and any siblings?'

'Why do you think they would have adopted me out?'

'Adoptions are done in either the mother's or baby's best interest, so it is probably best to approach this unknown situation cautiously. Adoptions can be the result of teenage pregnancies or mothers getting mental illnesses like post-natal psychosis after childbirth. There are many reasons, like catastrophic maternity emergencies impacting on the mother's health. How about we make an appointment to see the social worker?'

'Actually, I spoke to a social worker called Annie today. She gave me information about the Adoption and Permanent Care services. Annie said that I can get information about my birth parents and siblings there and apply for other social and medical information. I am sorry for being such a wimp.'

'I will help you as much as I can. I have Sunday off, so let's check out the online applications together.'

'I don't want Dad to know. I don't want to hurt him or have Dad think he's not enough.'

'Jack would want you to do what makes you happy, yet his health may be a bit too susceptible to cope with changes just now. Let's take this a day at a time.'

'I can see my dad was blessed when he met you,' Taylor said.

'Jack's always said his life was brightened immensely when you and Michelle came along. He has loved you for twenty-eight years, and Jack will continue to until the day he dies.'

Taylor kissed her cheek, then turned away to wipe

the tears spilling down his face. At least Taylor's intake of beers was slowing, as he was processing rather than trying to chemically escape his fears.

Chapter Ten
Kylie and Taylor

'*N*ow that we know that I regressed today to a sookie la-la, how did you spend your day?' Taylor asked, trying to instil humour after the heavy dialogue.

'Oh, I just helped out the father of one of my friends with some of his work contracts,' Kylie answered.

'Doing what?' Taylor questioned, wanting to thank Kylie for the maintenance she did on his father's house.

'When I went to uni, my friend Sally and I worked with her father, Bill, in the holidays to earn some money. When he gets more work than he can handle, Sally and I still periodically help him out. These days, Sally and I get spoilt by Bill giving us the lighter work inside.'

'What doing?'

'Oh, just minor renovations. Sally and I have worked together with Bill for about ten years. He knows that we are reliable. Bill likes not having to stand over us explaining plans.'

'Did you do Dad's back door? I went around there today, and it was fixed.'

'Yeah.'

'Thank you. And his jamming window was fixed too, I noticed.'

'Guilty as charged,' confessed Kylie.

'And there were baked home cooked meals, dated and labelled in the fridge.'

'Oh, they were just a few of his favourites. I sometimes went over on the weekends to keep an eye on Jack. We got the ingredients on the Thursday when we went shopping to make whatever Jack was craving on the Saturday. Jack and I made them together, so his food had just the right salt or sauce flavours he liked. I put fresh, chopped up kale, spinach, grated zucchini and carrots into every dish to keep him healthy. I will let you guess who was busily adding all the honey.'

Kylie and Taylor both smiled, while looking into each other's eyes.

'You are very kind, Kylie. Dad and I truly appreciate everything you have done for us. Now I feel even guiltier about how I mistreated you when we first met.'

'I will always feel terribly ashamed about Jack ending up in Intensive Care. I wish I could have persuaded him to go into twenty-four-hour residential care. At least now, unless he has deteriorated, we can accommodate Jack staying at home.'

'Dad wanted to stay at home, and you tried to support that wish. I intend to make this all up to you, Kylie. You are amazing,' Taylor said, taking hold of her tiny, calloused hands.

'Taylor, you need to take the opportunity for a break while you are home, rather than worry about everything. Honestly, what I did for Jack was my pleasure. Everything is fine. Let's just focus on getting Jack home.'

Changing the subject, Taylor asked, 'Do you mind if I ask whose room I stay in?'

'Timmy's. He comes back every three months. He always changes his linen before he leaves. Don't worry; I will wash the sheets before he gets back.'

'He seems to have a small build, going by the shirts hung up in his cupboard.'

'Yeah, Timmy has a small physique like me. He's only nineteen years old, but he's all muscle, so he's a bit heavier, probably about 65 kg.'

'I just wanted to make sure you don't have a boyfriend who's going to throw me out on my ear,' Taylor continued, probing.

'Low risk there,' Kylie evaded.

'Why's that?'

'It's just me, my brother and Hayley living there. Timmy's as gentle as a lamb.'

'Where is Timmy?'

'He's away at uni at the moment. Timmy should be home in about six weeks. He is studying a Bachelor of

Education. He wants to be a primary school teacher.'

'So, you are single then? Not dating anyone?'

'No.'

'I would like to date you, Kylie, if I can get my act together after these dramas. How would you feel about that?'

'We'll see. Can I be honest and suggest that you have enough going on right now? I don't feel that you are in the right head space for any more turmoil than you already have. In emotionally challenging situations like you are experiencing at the moment, psychologists usually recommend controlling changes for about six months. Can we ... maybe settle for a close friendship initially with a view to a relationship later on? How about just kisses, cuddles and emotional support rather than intimacy for those six months while you are under so much pressure? Most successful relationships begin as friendships.'

'I appreciate your honesty. I hope you don't think I'm this emotional normally. I must seem incredibly sensitive to you at the moment. We have met during one of the worst personal crises I have experienced in my life.'

'You're very hard on yourself, Taylor. You're allowed to be human. For your sake, I feel that I need to be wary of Jack's outcome, that still remains uncertain at his age and with a chronic lung condition. The adoption investigations you are embarking on are another huge emotional upheaval for you, too. Right now, you need baby steps. By that, I mean limiting changes. To cope with all this turmoil, you need to put the brakes on anything else that will cause you unnecessary additional anxiety.'

'I feel a bit too human at the moment. Raw and broken,' Taylor said, finishing up his drink. 'Don't worry, I won't burden you with my turbulent life. I asked you to date me because I like you.'

'For a non-drinker, you've had quite a few. Can I ask why you are single?'

'I am sorry about overindulging. I don't need you seeing me crash and burn. I was engaged just over five years ago. My fiancée, Heidi, was killed suddenly in a hit-and-run accident involving a drunk driver.'

Taylor sat silently, thinking about how much he still missed his beautiful fiancée. All their shared future plans were suddenly abandoned with her death. He had not sought another partner after that. Taylor had felt as though his body had been in tune with Heidi's. He had not even felt a return of his libido until now.

'Oh, I am sorry to hear that, Taylor! No judgement here about the drinking. Some events like bereavement and critical illnesses have to be navigated a day at a time. Jack's recovery will be like that. Can you get extra leave if Jack takes longer to progress at his age?'

'Yes, I am on family leave at the moment. I can either extend the family leave or take annual leave. God, I feel a mess.' Taylor shook his head in frustration. 'You're right, I should not have added alcohol to my woes. I was trying to numb my mind for a bit.'

'Unfortunately, alcohol is notorious for lowering your mood rather than elevating it. You don't have to go through this alone, Taylor. I can help you if you want.'

Taylor, still holding Kylie's tiny, roughened hand, brought her folded knuckles to his lips.

'You have done so much for Dad and me already. You are so lovely, Kylie. I like being around you.' Taylor leant over to kiss Kylie tenderly on her lips. 'I am not usually a weak, dependent person. I feel so exhausted and apprehensive at the moment.'

'Taylor, don't be afraid of changes,' Kylie suggested. 'Changes help us to grow psychologically to develop resilience. In many instances, opportunity is often disguised as loss. We learn more about ourselves during these transformations. It's strange, isn't it, how we all can be so strong and yet so vulnerable, depending on the circumstances. In Jack's case, it makes us both feel helpless that we can only offer him limited support.'

Taylor only released Kylie's hand temporarily to pay the bill. He entwined his fingers in hers again as they wandered out to her car. The more he saw of Kylie, the more attracted to her he became.

In Kylie's unit, Taylor knew he should say goodnight. Instead, he lingered. Not tired after sleeping the morning away, Kylie put on the television and flipped on the switch for the kettle.

'Would you like a cuppa?'

'Yes,' said Taylor, feeling restless. 'I don't feel like going to bed just yet.'

'There is a good movie on tonight, if you like Robert De Niro. Or we could watch something else,' suggested Kylie, thinking the humour in *Flawless* might help Taylor's mindset.

'Yes, that's a good idea. A movie might help take my mind off my troubles. Without work to distract me, I seem to be ruminating far too much.'

'We could see Jack tomorrow morning first thing, then try to get his car battery charged and the car started.'

'Are you mechanically minded too?'

'No, unfortunately I'm not. I know just the basics about car maintenance, I'm afraid. We can call the RACQ or book Jack's car in for a service.'

'Yes, it will probably need it. If Dad has early dementia, I imagine it will be a while since he has driven it.'

Kylie instantly blushed and dropped her head. 'I have both of Jack's car key sets here,' she confessed. 'That was another reason I brought you back here.'

Kylie retrieved them from her dressing table drawer.

'Originally when he was getting confused, I hid them at Jack's in a spare room cupboard, in a pocket of your jacket. Then I worried so much I ended up just taking them with me until I spoke to you. I was worried that Jack would try to drive, get confused and have an accident.'

'Hey, that's fine. I understand that. I also totally get that Dad was not wanting to leave home. It seems like you spent a lot of your own time trying to protect Dad and keep him safe.'

'Jack is so full of character. I love his friendly, easygoing personality. Jack is so easily pleased. I find all his little antics are endearing.'

'Yes, I love Dad dearly. As you say, if I had to be adopted, God chose well.'

'He did.'

'I have no right to be upset. It is Dad who is sick.'

'I did not mean that you don't have a right to be distraught at distressing news that has changed your whole concept of who you are.'

'I need a break from these raw emotions and endless possible scenarios revolving endlessly in my mind,' Taylor said, wiping his leaking eyes yet again.

Kylie embraced him as they stood in the kitchen. With her strong hands pressing firmly into his taut thoracic back muscles and Kylie's breath warm on his sternum, Taylor broke out in a laugh, retreating from her embrace.

'God, this is so embarrassing!' Taylor's body physically reacted again to the only female he had held in years. 'It seems I am to experience every emotion tonight,' he helplessly smirked, trying to hide his attraction. 'Now you are affecting me.'

Kylie stilled, staring intently at his groin. A red rash climbed her neck before she realised and quickly turned back to the kettle. Taylor released the laundry door, pleased that Hayley's scratching had broken the silence. Uncertain of what to do, he played ball with Hayley and started playing tug of war with her furry toy. Hayley greeted Kylie with a frantic patter.

As they settled in the lounge to watch their movie, Hayley lay across both laps, wagging her reverberating tail. Taylor clasped Kylie's warm hand.

While he was genuinely attracted to the cute nurse, Taylor heeded her caution about adding potential relationship dramas to his conflicted emotions. All Taylor could think about was the intense ache in his chest stemming from a desire he had not felt for ages. After their dinner conversation, Taylor found himself grieving and missing Heidi all over again, yet, bizarrely, he sought the comfort of Kylie's body. What a mess!

Taylor placed his right arm around Kylie's shoulders on the lounge, wanting her nearer. Kylie nestled into him, her warm touch arousing him again. When Taylor reached to place a cushion discreetly over his lap, he found Kylie's blue eyes curiously focused there again. Kylie looked up at him, wide-eyed and speechless. He had noticed Kylie looking at his T-shirt stretched firmly over his chest and his defined arm muscles. This morning, she had been diverted watching his legs when he wore shorts. Kylie had stared too often at Taylor for him to ignore the longing in her eyes. Yet rather than fuelling the fire, she had tried to refocus him. What a conundrum!

Taylor sensed a slight tugging of his shirt. Kylie had undone a shirt button at his waist and was placing her tiny hand on his hairy abs. He gasped at its coldness.

Usually, Kylie had only looked at him when she thought Taylor was not paying attention. This was the first time Kylie had touched him that was not out of pity. The splay of her rough hands combing his coarse abdominal hair sent a chemical shock through him that was not helping his arousal. Hayley jumped up from their legs and mouthed Kylie's hand through his beige linen shirt as though it was a game.

'She thinks I'm playing doona monsters,' chuckled Kylie. 'I usually put my hands under my doona to start a game.'

'I'd like to play doona monsters too,' flirted Taylor, looking down at her intimate contact. 'I hope I get my turn.'

He kissed the top of Kylie's head before looking back at the movie. Kylie's hand migrated slightly upwards to the thicker chest hair centred at his sternum. Losing interest, Hayley dropped down on her paws and snoozed. Taylor inhaled deeply, enjoying the feather touch of Kylie's exploration as she raked her fingers through his chest hair. His mood became elevated by the humorous movie.

When Kylie's hand stilled and relaxed, Taylor looked down to find her eyelids fluttering. Her breathing deepened as she melted her warm body against him. When the movie ended, Taylor gently placed Hayley on the floor. He tenderly stroked Kylie's hair to waken her. Emerging from the effort of leaving a deep sleep, her eyelids struggled open.

'Can we continue this cuddle in one of our rooms?' Taylor questioned.

Kylie stretched and yawned. 'Okay. I will need five minutes to get into my pyjamas, though.'

'Absolutely. Cuddling you has been so lovely. I am enjoying it. I don't want this moment to end.' With a hand resting on her lower back, he gently drew her in closer.

'Five minutes. You can change and come into my room.' Kylie said, breaking from Taylor's embrace. 'Bring your pillow.'

With Kylie's back and soft bottom spooned against him, both soon dozed off.

Chapter Eleven
Sally and Greg

*I*n the following month, Sally and Greg worked few shifts together. When they were on the same shift, Sally either spent the shift helping another nurse with a new admission that was unstable or had many medical emergencies in the wards to attend to.

When Greg asked for Sally's address to pick her up for the airport, he was keen to learn more about her. Greg arrived at the small, pale brick house with a pale green roof and brown trims to find her waiting outside on the patio. After lifting her luggage into his boot, they took off in Greg's Pajero to make their flight.

During their lunch together in Sydney, Greg thought it was odd that Sally had taken herself off to the bathroom not long after leaving the motel. Sally had ordered a diet lemon, lime and bitters canned drink while Greg had indulged in a holiday beer. Greg wondered why she was ordering diet soft drinks when Sally looked far from needing weight loss strategies.

'So, where shall we spend the afternoon? Do you like to hit the shops?'

The way Sally's expressive blue eyes instantly lit up left Greg in no doubt. Sally grinned widely, her smile lighting up her gorgeous face.

'Yes, let's start with some fragrances.'

Greg had sniffed the coffee beans offered between each spray. As he sniffed her wrist and forearm after each floral fragrance, he felt the electric sensation of touching Sally's skin arc right through him. In the male section of the department store, Sally sprayed woodier scents and citrusy smells all over him. At one stage, she sprayed at his neck. As Sally leaned in to smell the men's cologne, her soft breath as she inhaled left him aroused. Thank God he could hide behind her purchases.

'I think we need to move on soon before you leave me smelling like a brothel,' Greg teased. It's nearly 2 pm. We can come back after we get our conference bags and events tickets if you like.'

'Hmmm, let's come back and look at clothes. I need a dress for Saturday night's gala. Did you get your outfit yet?'

'Yes. I was not sure how much sightseeing you planned to be doing, so I just hired a suit.'

After booking in and collecting their conference tickets, Sally tried on a wispy navy, light blue and grey chiffon dress with a swirling black glittering print.

Greg could not take his eyes off how the fabric clung to her feminine curves, seductively enveloping her body. Worse still, he struggled to peel his eyes off the V-neckline that revealed her generous cleavage. Sally raised her eyes from the garment to find him looking like a starstruck teenager. Greg moved the shopping bags in front of himself. He'd placed a jacket in his conference bag, intending to carry it everywhere they went to avoid embarrassment. As Sally twirled around to show Greg the back view, she found his mouth gaping.

'Stunning, absolutely stunning! You look gorgeous,' he answered honestly.

Sally stopped mid-twirl, recognising the sincerity there. She smiled coyly at Greg. He was besotted!

'Now, do you have black shoes suitable for dancing?' Greg questioned, struggling to raise his eyes. 'I intend to have you twirling like that around the dance floor.'

'Yes, it was just a dress I needed.'

After their evening meal of a seafood banquet in a restaurant ambiently lit with table candles, Greg sighed and stretched.

'I'm stuffed. That was so tasty.'

'Yes. I love prawns, especially crumbed. I always consider it sacrilegious to batter a prawn or scallop. I loved the salad and the tartare. Everything was cooked to perfection.'

'The company was amazing, too.'

Sally looked up into Greg's honey brown eyes,

uncertain how to respond.

'What will we do tomorrow evening?' she asked uncertainly, changing the subject.

'Are we going to the zoo or the Queen Victoria Building?'

'Would you like to get the ferry to the zoo? If we have time, we could then go to Manly.'

'Yes. Let's take our jackets and joggers, in case it rains.'

Once again, Greg's attention was curiously drawn to Sally getting a diet soft drink and no alcohol as they dined out.

'You don't drink alcohol?'

'No, it makes me feel too sluggish.'

'I only have the odd beer on holidays or a night out. It relaxes me.'

'You cannot feel relaxed without alcohol?'

'I can. I just enjoy the odd beer and charming company more.'

He noticed how regimented Sally was in what she digested and the times she ate. At work, Sally always ate her main meals at 6 am, midday, 6 pm or midnight, depending on what shift she was working. Even on her days off and on holidays now, Greg noticed that Sally rigidly adhered to that schedule.

He was enjoying spending so much time with her. Even though Sally wore a brunch coat over her pyjamas, even just glimpses of her slim legs and bare feet with frosty pink painted toenails were appealing.

Friday morning as planned, Sally sat at the breakfast

conference. Instead of snacks like bacon and egg wraps and appetisers being available prior to the talk, the food was only available at the end of the lecture. Greg felt Sally slumping over towards him and noticed her clumsily rubbing her eyes. Sally's vision blurred as her forehead rapidly bubbled in sweat. Sally placed a diaphoretic hand on Greg, trying to tell him to get something out of her bag. Her mind and body seemed disconnected, before Sally slid off the conference seat as blackness enveloped her. She was incontinent.

At first, Greg had assumed that Sally was leaning into him to whisper something. The next thing, she was grossly uncoordinated and unable to talk. Greg quickly grabbed Sally's shirt at the last minute to stop her falling. She was a dead weight as he lowered her to the ground.

'Help! Help! Someone, call an ambulance!' Greg called, shocked. He began rolling the unconscious Sally onto her side.

'What's happened?' asked an intensivist seated on the other side of Greg.

'I don't know. Sally was fine when we left the motel room this morning. She said she was hungry and looking forward to breakfast.'

'Is she pregnant?' the doctor asked, feeling her pulse.

'Not that I am aware of.'

The male doctor automatically reverted to problem solving, using the Hs and Ts of emergencies. Greg knew he was ticking them off in his mind.

She's not hypoxic: the lady has plenty of oxygen, she's breathing well, and her lips are not blue. Any renal failure history? As regards potassium levels being high or low as in hyper- or hypokalaemia, her pulse is strong and rapid.

'She must be diabetic,' the intensivist asserted. 'This lady is very clammy and initially had slurred speech. It could be either hypoglycaemia or hypotension. See if any sales reps can get us a glucose monitoring machine and sphygmomanometer to measure her blood pressure This loss of consciousness was sudden. Her pulse is strong and regular, so it does not seem likely to be an arrhythmia. There are only unlikely scenarios to go: tension pneumothorax, tamponade, temperature, thrombosis or toxins.'

Greg raced back from the medical displays, anxiously dragging a salesman in tow carrying a glucose monitor and an automated blood pressure device.

'This lady seems to be symptomatic of low blood sugar.'

Greg discovered the intensivist checking Sally's handbag for toxins in the form of medications or illicit drugs. Greg looked on stunned as the doctor extracted a navy-blue insulin pen.

'Did she have an injection this morning?'

'I don't know,' Greg replied, looking bewildered. 'We are staying at the same motel but in separate rooms. Sally had mentioned something about expecting to eat first and look at the displays.'

Sally remained motionless with no withdrawal reaction to her fingertip being pricked on the side.

'She is deeply unresponsive,' the doctor noted.

A critical value of 1.4 millimoles per litre (mmol/L) was displayed on the glucometer screen, well below the minimum safe level of 4 mmol/L. Her urine was puddled underneath her.

'Does anyone have a medical kit here?' the doctor shouted. 'We need glucagon or an intravenous line with glucose Stat!'

Another sales rep rushed over with a glucagon minijet extracted from a Thomas Pack belonging to the Royal Flying Doctors' emergency equipment exhibit.

'Thanks,' the doctor replied before injecting Sally with the emergency glucagon minijet.

A second glucose measurement was recorded at 2.3 mmol/L. With Sally remaining deeply unconscious, her oral secretions were draining out of her flaccid mouth. After the glucagon injection, as Sally's five-minutely blood sugar levels climbed to 2.8, she began thrashing. With her brain not having its normal carbohydrate fuel, as Sally's sugar level improved, she became confused and slightly agitated. Another glucagon was administered to obtain a 4.2 mmol/L reading at fifteen minutes. Although pale, Sally began opening her eyes just as the paramedics arrived.

'Sally, your blood sugar level went too low,' Greg explained, placing his hands gently on her damp face to get her attention. An intravenous cannula was inserted and an intravenous ten per cent dextrose infusion was commenced at 50 ml per hour. Sally was strapped to the gurney in a lateral position for transport to Royal North Shore Hospital.

'Sally, I will bring some clothes and toiletries to the hospital for you,' Greg mentioned, holding her hand.

He kissed her on the forehead, staring at her sallow drooping face. Greg placed Sally's handbag on the trolley with her, alerting the paramedics to the presence of her insulin inside.

'I did not know Sally was diabetic,' Greg explained to the ambulance officer. 'She may have administered her insulin in the motel room before we left, because she was expecting to eat breakfast on arrival. However, as soon as we got here, the lecture began before any food was offered.'

Greg left the breakfast lecture, heading for their room. He searched Sally's room to collect her pyjamas, underwear and toiletries to take to the hospital. Distraught from seeing Sally lying so lifeless, Greg took several deep breaths to quell his panic.

Suddenly, it all made sense! Sally's rigid eating routines, diet soft drinks and avoiding alcohol were not a choice.

'Think!' he said aloud to himself. 'What will Sally need?'

In the end, Greg packed a pair of black trousers, a top and a pair of shoes to wear home. He suspected the shoes Sally was wearing would need a rinse. Greg placed everything he'd collected into a plastic shopping bag and found a second plastic bag to separate the wet clothes she was wearing.

By the time Greg made it to the hospital, Sally was being admitted to the twenty-four-hour observation ward. It broke his heart to see her looking so humiliated.

'How are you feeling?' Greg asked, concerned.

'Fine,' Sally said, her head dropped, focusing on her fingers to avoid eye contact.

Her pale face looked a ghostly image of its former vibrant self. Greg sat down and began by holding her hand, unsure how to approach Sally in the awkward silence that followed. Sally was gutted. She looked defeated, ashamed and virtually buried in the "one size fits nobody" hospital gown. Greg stood up to place her underwear and clothes in the locker. He scooped the ammonia scented clothes Sally had been wearing into the second plastic bag to wash in the bathtub back at the motel. Greg tied the handles of the plastic bag with the dirty clothes in and left it at his feet to take with him when he left.

'I'm so sorry,' Sally suddenly gushed. Her sad blue eyes were instantly buried in her small hands as she covered her face.

'Hey, hey!' Greg soothed, brushing Sally's curly bob away from her flushed face. 'I'm just glad that you are okay.' Greg leaned over, planting a soft kiss on Sally's forehead. 'You gave me quite a fright. I've been terribly worried about you!'

'I'm stuck here for four hours of observation now,' Sally grimaced.

'That's okay,' Greg mollified her. 'I'm happy as long as you are doing okay. That is all that matters.'

'I've ruined this morning's conference for you. I am so sorry.' Sally's nervous forced smile was fading.

'You've ruined nothing, Sally! I could be at the conference still if I had wanted to remain there. I chose to be here with you. It is important to me that you are safe and well. In four hours,' Greg said, checking his watch, 'you might still catch that Belgian doctor's lecture you wanted to hear, if you're feeling up to it. Otherwise, we might ask if we can have a recording of the talk or a copy of his published article; usually, the PowerPoint rules of five words and five rows make the speech recordings more useful. Right now, that is not important. I am here for you. You are all that matters.'

'I feel so stupid. I did not want to keep going to the loo all the time when I was with you. So I tried to take my insulin before we went to the breakfast. I put two biscuits in my bag and carried jellybeans too, just in case. The hypoglycaemia came on so suddenly I could not get them out of my bag. I could not even talk properly.'

'Sally, you don't need to hide anything from me. I care very much about you. You don't have to hide your diabetes. I wish you would have told me, that's all. I could have helped you more immediately if I had known.'

'I did not want to be a burden or make you feel that you

were still working,' Sally tearfully rationalised.

'Sally, I enjoy your company. You are no burden. I care about you.'

Greg picked up her hand to kiss her knuckles. This time, he did not let her rough calloused hand go as he resumed sitting on the chair again. Sally anxiously watched him closely, searching intently for signs of disapproval. What she found was sincerity. Greg chewed his lower lip, seeking to change the subject. He desperately wanted Sally to relax.

'If you get out on bail, we could just have a swim this afternoon, if you like.'

'Yes, we'll see what happens. Thank you for being so supportive.'

'Hey, you have dug me out of deep shit often enough, Sally Price. I don't know how many times you have helped me problem solve or stopped me making mistakes. Every shift I work with you, you always help whoever has the heaviest workload.'

Greg looked into her eyes. 'Can I give you a hug? You look like you need one.'

Sally nodded. Greg stood to embrace her, not wanting to let go. While he was still holding her, Greg bent to kiss her forehead.

'So, spill. How long have you been diabetic?'

'Since I was six years old. I remember breathing really fast, drinking a lot and still feeling very thirsty all the time. I was finally diagnosed after I wet myself in front of my whole class. I was absolutely mortified when all the kids laughed.'

'That would have been embarrassing for you! Children that age wouldn't understand the seriousness behind what was happening.'

'I ended up admitted to the Intensive Care Unit with a sugar level off the scale. The first reading was calculated at 54 mmol/L. Although the nurses were lovely and caring, I hated the needles. The needles felt like self-mutilation. However, I complied with the injections to avoid being incontinent in public again. To be honest, I am studying to get into education. I am struggling with shiftwork and circadian rhythm disturbances, causing my body to produce stress hormones that fluctuate my sugar levels. That is why my endocrinologist, Dr Jacobs, always greets me so warmly.'

'Why have you kept it a secret?'

'I don't want pity from others. Dr Jacobs told me life is managed, not lived. If I want a healthy life, I need to control my symptoms by being disciplined and managing the diabetes mellitus myself. Usually at the conferences, you see the displays before the lectures. I just got it wrong this morning and stuffed up big time.'

'You're fine, honey. You are doing well. Your condition does not change how I feel about you. I like you a lot – a hell of a lot! I don't even want to let go of you now, to be truthful.'

'It's this sexy purple hospital gown I'm drowning in, am I right?' Sally jested.

Looking her directly in the eye, Greg softly said, 'Among many other things.'

'Well, it can't be these disposable hospital knickers.'

Clutching his chest, Greg responded, 'Be still, my beating heart.'

He laughed, pretending to lift her nightie. Sally swatted his hands away playfully.

'You're shocking!' She laughed.

'Besotted,' Greg clarified. 'I have watched you for eighteen months from a distance. Now that I have permission, I don't want to let you go.'

Greg sat again, holding her hand while the intravenous fluids continued to infuse.

'Why did you wait eighteen months if you felt so strongly about wanting to be with me? I was never clear, when you asked me to go somewhere, about whether you were organising ICU events or interested in me.'

'Well, my attraction to you was instant. But my hesitation was having a relationship with someone I work with. I did not want that to get awkward.'

'Awkward? How?'

'If it did not work out, relationship breakdowns can be destructive in the workplace. We both like working in ICU. I promise you, though, I will always treat you with respect. I was hoping you might give me a chance.'

'Greg, I am just living my life a day at a time at the moment. I'm struggling with shiftwork and my diabetes. I am studying my master's to get into an educator role, hopefully in ICU. I can't promise you anything. I am sorry.'

'All I am asking is that you share that day at a time with me, Sally Price. I truly care for you. I was hoping to ask you on the plane on the way home if you would date me, after we had an enjoyable conference holiday together.'

'One day at a time is all I can do. If I cannot get into an educator role, I might need to drop shifts.'

'Then let me help you. Let me look after you a little, Sally.' Greg swept the curly hair falling into her face behind her ear before continuing. 'I would enjoy nothing more than spoiling you. I won't get in the way of your study or career plans.'

'You don't need to be drawn into my circus at the moment.'

'Sally, I am right where I want to be. I am here because I care for you very much. Do you have any feelings for me at all?'

'We have always got along well, Greg. I trust you. I do feel an attraction for you. I had not allowed myself to believe that you were interested in me. I thought you were always organising ICU social events and just trying to include me. It is the timing I worry about. When I get an educator role, it would not be as awkward for others with us working together.'

'It can be our secret, Sally. Please, let's take this a day at a time, with no pressure.'

'Okay, I'd like that,' Sally replied, reaching for Greg's hand. Heaving a sigh of relief, Greg bent forward for another hug. *Thank God*, he thought. Together, they waited at the hospital until Sally was discharged at 1 pm.

'Now, there will be no need to be racing to the toilet to inject your insulin while you are with me when you are not at work. We could even see if you can get a glucagon minijet for me to administer in an emergency,' Greg suggested. 'You tell me when you are tired, and we can go back to our room together.'

'One day at a time,' Sally reminded Greg. 'I could not bear it if I upset you. At the moment, I cannot cope with more stress.'

'I am here to support you, Sally. I will not be judging you or pressuring you. I just need you to tell me if you are tired or feeling down. If you want – and this is just a thought – while we are at the conference, we could have a look at those new implantable insulin pumps with their clever algorithms. I will support you in whatever direction you choose to go.'

'Let's catch that one-hour lecture at the conference then.'

'I can't wait. Then you can decide if you want to go to our room for a rest, or if you would like that swim.'

'Deal.'

Back in their room, Sally invited Greg to relax on her bed while she took an evening nap.

'I'll be there in five minutes,' he replied.

Greg washed Sally's urine drenched clothes with soap and hung them up in the shower recess to dry. Fully dressed, they both lay together, chatting and cuddling. Totally relaxed, Sally drifted off to sleep, breathing deeply and rhythmically. With her hair fanned out loose on her pillow, she looked beautiful. Greg lay there, euphoric at the progress he had made.

Chapter Twelve

Becoming a new couple

*K*ylie drove Taylor over to Jack's house after their hospital visit to see if Jack's car battery was flat and whether the vehicle needed a service.

'Look,' said Kylie, pointing excitedly at Jack's fence. 'There are two crows there! That may mean that Jack will be coming home. To the animal spirit guide, crows mean transformation. Every animal has a positive and a negative aspect to their nature. Bees, for example, make honey, but they can also sting. With crows, the number is significant as well. Two crows means luck.'

'Well, I do hope that interpretation is right. I would love to spend time at home with Dad.'

'When you receive messages from the spirit world, we are just meant to acknowledge them and appreciate the communication,' Kylie explained. 'It is reassurance. It does not matter if you cannot always decipher the message. The spirit world is telling you that you are supported.'

'Let's take Dad's car for a drive.'

'Yes. It has not been driven for two weeks. That was the last time I drove him to the shops.'

Taylor turned the key in the switch. The old Holden sedan chugged a bit before it idled.

'What do you say to us getting some petrol and going to the beach?'

'Why not?' Kylie said, grabbing her handbag.

'I find driving very relaxing,' Taylor added. 'I like getting out in the patterns of nature when I'm not on duty.'

'We could stop back home and grab some togs and towels.'

'Good idea. I don't have swimmers, but I could change into shorts.'

Taylor looked at the sky, admiring the beautiful warm day. The sky was a clear blue with the odd puffy, white cumulus cloud reflecting sunlight. Perfect for a swim, he hoped.

At the beach, they parked Jack's car and strolled along a sandy track through shady forest canopy that opened to reveal a panoramic ocean view. Dropping their towels and clothes on the warm sand, Taylor found himself gasping at the sight of Kylie in her bathing suit after she'd shrugged off her shirt and shorts. Her long hair was flowing over her shoulders and periodically swept into her face by the sea breeze. Kylie looked up to discover him awestruck, staring at her blue, white, green and pink floral bikini.

Blimey, Taylor thought to himself, *seeing her in her togs is just as enticing as viewing her in those short cotton pyjamas.* Showing remarkable discipline, Taylor moved his eyes up to Kylie's face, as she dropped her discarded clothes into her sports bag, but not before appreciating her flat belly and narrow waist. Awestruck, Kylie sneaked a peek at Taylor's hirsute chest, sculptured biceps and six-pack abdomen as he removed his shirt.

They wandered down towards the hard, wet sand, inhaling the salty ocean breeze. Nervous seagulls scattered along the shoreline, looking up from foraging food. The foaming white line of the waves came towards them as they stepped into the cool tidal water.

'You look like you really work out,' Kylie said with admiration after she was caught perving.

'Yes, self-preservation requires us to move quickly and stay fit.'

'I suppose safety is one of the things we Australians who have never seen action take for granted.'

'Sometimes, if you have too many missions that are dangerous back-to-back, it can make us soldiers quite paranoid. You tend to overreact to loud noises or startle at strange noises.'

'That would be traumatic.'

'In war zones, you often don't know who to trust either. You often find it hard to identify who is friend and who is foe. So, you trust no one, not even women and children.'

Taking Kylie's hand, they entered the surf together. Kylie gasped as the first spray of cool ocean water hit her bare waist. Taylor released her hand to dive into the surf.

'Come in further. It's great.'

Kylie responded by swimming over, keeping her head out of the water, as she adjusted to the cooler temperature.

'Coming to the beach was a great idea,' Kylie commented.

She found herself staring, fascinated at his hairy chest.

'I just wanted to spend some quality time with you away from the hospital. Being in your company keeps my mind off this adoption news that has been plaguing me. I was already feeling guilty about not being home as much as I wanted to be for Dad. That regret was compounded by Dad's critical illness coming out of the blue after a six-month intense mission. I was unprepared for more major changes. So the Young's syndrome news just kind of rattled my cage and tipped me over the edge further. After hearing that news, I suddenly felt like an alien. I began doubting who I am. It was like I was living in a world where I no longer felt like I belonged. My mind seems to be manifesting demons that I cannot deal with right now.'

'While I don't know the nature of the mission you were on, you are certainly processing a lot in your civilian life right now. It is easy to understand why you feel uneasy.'

'I feel lost. Empty. Exasperated even. My whole sense of self seems distorted.'

'Hopefully, you will get to meet your biological parents, if they are willing. I think the best mindset is not to have any expectations. There is no guarantee that you will get any questions answered. This situation is like a pendulum where the worst possible scenario is that no one is willing to meet with you. In that case, you've lost nothing. You've had an amazing life with Jack and Michelle, and as you said, God could not have chosen better.'

'I intend to proceed carefully and not tell Dad. I don't want to offend him or have him think that he and Mum were not enough. I would just really appreciate learning a little more about my history.'

'It is vital that all Jack's energy goes into healing for now. It is essential that he does not worry about anything. Jack was watching your facial expressions when you were frowning. He knows you are worried and not your usual self, but he has no clue about why. I think Jack would be surprised that you forgot. Jack loves you very much.'

'I love Dad, too. As you said, I was probably told and had a child's short attention span. I probably did not really understand the importance of what was being said. My day-to-day life was unchanged, so I could have forgotten.'

'To a child, the significance of news is often interpreted by the amount of major upheaval. If you think about what children go through during a divorce, it is often heralded by parents separating, children moving house and having to attend different schools. In your case, you may not have understood what adopted meant. The new information, that your parents must have believed you integrated, did not disrupt your daily routines. Everything remained constant. You were loved, cared for and there was no turmoil. You felt safe and a member of a doting family.'

'I was very young.'

'Your parents always considered you their son. There were no custody battles or events to suggest otherwise. Home is where the heart is. Now, you may have extra parents, possibly another family, depending on what contact your biological parents consent to. Each party gets to determine how much they participate in the journey.'

'I feel anxious about this unknown future, but I would really appreciate learning a little more about my history.'

'Sometimes when we get stressed, our minds tend to catastrophise, looking at the worst extremes. Alternatively, there could be a whole new world opening up to you of biological parents, siblings and cousins. So, I'm encouraging you to have no expectations whatsoever. As the saying goes, "What is, is!" Don't forget that you get to determine what contact you are comfortable with, too. It is important that you don't feel powerless. Keep reminding yourself that you will have some control over what happens next.'

Taylor cradled Kylie in the water with his thick arms wrapped around her tiny narrow shoulders.

'Thank you again for sharing your honest perspective. You are helping to ground me during this havoc. You're the reality check I need at the moment. Your sensitive and professional advice is helping to level me.'

'Life is a journey of hills, roundabouts, traffic lights, storms, celebrations. For you, military life is about being disciplined and reacting to situations. However, life teaches you that remaining healthy requires flexibility. Part of the journey into adulthood, too, is recognising that we always have choices.'

'I can see why my father would benefit from living with you if we can get him home.'

'Jack is loads of fun. He has such a welcoming personality. Jack knows what he likes and is not hard to please. It would be my pleasure to live in his house until you get your holidays. We will need to synchronise our holidays, though.'

'You would still keep your unit?'

'Yes, my brother Timmy would need somewhere to live during his uni holidays. I would want to give you and Jack alone time, too.'

'Where are your parents, Kylie?'

'My dad is dead. He died suddenly of an asthma attack when he got influenza about two years ago. My mother left, abandoning us when we were young. So, there is just Timmy and me. We get along fabulously. We support each other.'

'That must be hard.'

'Not at all. Timmy is the ideal little brother. He is intelligent, helpful, funny.'

'No, I mean not having parents.'

'Dad was very loving and caring. He gave us the best life he could afford. My mother left us because she was exasperated about never having enough money or choices. With their mortgage, they barely struggled to pay the bills each payday. Neither Timmy nor I have ever had any need to search for her. She left us of her own choice, leaving Dad with the workload of two parents. Dad never complained. As we grew older, Timmy and I both chipped in with washing and cooking to ease Dad's workloads. Dad worked for Sally's father, Bill, in the early days when their business was starting up. Bill always looked out for us and gave us extra as the business grew. It is about loyalty, for Timmy and me. Timmy works for Bill on his holidays to earn money for his teaching degree. If Bill has too much work on, we all help out. We are a team. Bill's goodwill and the bonuses he paid Dad always got repaid in labour.'

'You make my life seem like I've been spoiled.'

'Not at all. Taylor, I am glad for every family where children grow up feeling loved and appreciated.'

'I definitely was. I should not be moaning about where I came from.'

'I think you need to accept that this is a very vulnerable time for you. You are allowed to be sensitive when so many changes are happening at once, especially when they are changes you have limited control over.'

Kylie hugged Taylor in the surf. With her firm, petite, half-naked body pressed against him, Taylor retreated a little. A forceful wave pushed Kylie into Taylor further, leaving her in no doubt about his desire for her.

'Well, you are certainly taking my mind off this situation,' Taylor flirted.

'That was not my original intention, but it's good. I think I was meant to come into your life right now to make sure you progress with more faith than fear.'

Trying to be a gentleman, Taylor tried moving his trunk backwards. His subsequent move to kiss Kylie's rosy lips escalated to them both engaged in a longing kiss. Taylor felt his passion igniting with each contact of her salty, satin skin. The taste of her kiss lingered. The urgent pressure of her rough strong hands on his back left an impression of intense need. Another wave swept her closer. Both soon became entangled while laughing breathlessly. As their bodies melted together in the surf, Taylor played with her smooth, silky, long tendrils of light brown hair, fanning out and undulating with the ocean's movement.

Kylie's gaze lingered on his biceps, admiring the defined, taut muscles holding her close. Kylie found his deep voice sexy. Being this close stimulated her with a restless energy. Kylie found herself excited immensely by the contact of his naked, hairy, buffed chest pressing against her breasts. She looked up at Taylor's bright green eyes, identifying his raw need. He had instantly transformed from having his spirit crushed to a new type of longing. A red flush washed up her neck to heat her cheeks. This turn of events was totally unexpected.

The cool indifference Taylor displayed when they had first met had now morphed into sheer lust. The firmness she felt at his proximity was not what he needed right now. Yet, this brittle soldier was powerless to hide his physical need. Taylor's hands began wandering over her slender feminine physique with erotic effect. He massaged every delicious curve of her delicate bone structure as though committing it to memory. Kylie entwined her hands in his, attempting to break the attachment beginning to overpower her.

'I'm not trying to confuse you, Taylor,' Kylie apologised but remained unable to stop herself from seeking more skin-to-skin contact with him. She let go of his hands and began raking her hands over his coarse chest hair, fascinated by its density and the bubbles trapped from the surf. Her touch of his erogenous nipple zones sent electricity bolts through him.

'Confuse me?' Taylor whispered, sighing deeply.

'This is not what you need right now. You have enough going on.'

Kylie released his hands, but the yearning and restlessness grew within her. She found herself spontaneously hugging and clinging helplessly to him again. Taylor stared at Kylie. She looked both conflicted with desire and incapable of restraint.

'You are feeling this yearning too, Kylie. This sensation is intense, isn't it?'

'Yes, but the timing is wrong. You don't need passion

and complications in your life right now.'

If the truth be known, she was lusting for more. She did not want to let him go. Her heart was filling her chest. The intimacy she felt radiating through her was beyond her capacity to resist. Kylie pressed her lips against his clean, shaven jaw, wanting more contact.

'You can stop me anytime, Kylie.'

'I wish I could,' she said, sounding defeated. 'This is not the right thing for you. It is a frustration you don't need,' she acknowledged, helpless to stop.

Uncertainty had her lusting for more contact with him. When Kylie's breasts pressed longingly into his chest again, his enticing biceps enclosed her small shoulders. Kylie's legs circled his waist in defeat, sending another electric buzz through him. As Taylor flashed her his charming grin, her resolve dissipated. The feather touch of his kisses on her neck became terrifyingly unrepentant.

'We shouldn't be doing this,' Kylie tried again.

'We are both single adults capable of giving consent,' Taylor rationalised in his sexy timbre.

'Yeah, but your emotions are everywhere right now. You don't need complications.'

'Kylie, you would be the cutest complication ever. I find you totally irresistible.'

Taylor looked longingly at Kylie, embracing her in another deep kiss that left her blissful. Kylie's warm body had him enthralled. Her soft hungry kisses fuelled his raging libido. The shiver of excitement built as he responded tenderly. Taylor's hands slid up and down the contours of her restless body. His heart was hammering in his chest.

'I'd rather these thoughts were etched into my memory,' he whispered, admiring her flawless, vibrant complexion. Taylor's cheek muscles begin to ache from smiling. How, in all this turmoil, could he feel this deliriously happy?

'Taylor...'

'Hmmm,' Taylor responded with smug amusement.

'I love your bear hugs.'

'Hmmm ... ditto.'

'And your touch is ... creating havoc ... with my moral landscape.'

'I hope so.'

He watched Kylie's face expressing fleeting emotions that ranged from flustered to eager and endearing to sensual. It was beyond his ability to rein her in.

"I'm not sure what the hell to do here,' Kylie admitted.

Her body was melting into his, enjoying their full chest contact. Her hands trailed up his coarse arm hairs to his shoulders.

'I vote for the thrill of surrender.'

Kylie fluttered her eyelashes but remained powerless to move.

'You are diverting my entire blood flow south,' he moaned, enveloping her with intense desire.

Kylie's tiny, rough hands curled, pressing with tension

into his shoulders.

'My heart and my body are craving more of you.'

Taylor stroked her back as though unable to stop. He felt seduced by her longing kisses. Her gentle touch was replaced with clinging pressure. Kylie seemed unwilling to disengage her chest from his. Since she first implanted her head in his chest, Kylie had him aching for her night and day. Taylor twirled her long hair affectionately, enjoying listening to her vocalise her guilty pleasures. Stupid with lust, amusement appeared in his sparkling eyes. Kylie was touching his sleek muscles as they flexed, rubbing gently up and down her back. His senses were totally off kilter.

'Where do we go from here?' Taylor rasped, nibbling on her ear lobe. Kylie's raw hunger egged him on.

'Home ... my home.'

'And should I buy some condoms?'

'No, there are some in Timmy's drawer.'

Kylie looked moony-eyed and relaxed.

'Timmy's drawer?'

'I put them there in case he could not control himself. I wanted to send him the message that if you have consent, it's okay to take precautions.'

'Hmmm, and do I have consent?' Taylor asked huskily, ravenous for more.

'Hmmm, my moral compass has encountered your profound magnetic force. I want to do the right thing. I know this is not what you need right now.'

Kylie groaned, squirming tensely against his hardness.

'Let's just take this journey together, shall we? Explore where this impulse is taking us.'

Taylor's mood shifted as his need to take her became torturous.

'I need to detach. But I cannot bear to peel away from you. You're like an addiction.'

Kylie took a deep breath reluctant to disengage. She was intensely drawn to him and desperate for more of his gentle touch.

Chapter Thirteen
Kylie's hesitation

*D*riving home in Jack's car, Taylor held Kylie's hand, rubbing his thumb over her tiny knuckles. She'd become quieter and had begun nibbling her fingernails on the opposite hand.

'Are you okay, honey? You look nervous.'

'I'm fine,' Kylie said, almost dismissively.

'Don't forget what you told me, Kylie. You have choices. We don't have to do anything when we get back to your place.'

'I gave my word, and I keep it,' she avowed.

'Kylie! This is not a business contract. I'm crazy about you! We won't proceed if you're uneasy.'

Kylie looked out the window. Something was not right. Taylor steered Jack's car onto the curb.

'What are you doing?' Kylie asked, alert.

'What is really the matter?'

Taylor looked over, uncertain. Since returning to Jack's car, Kylie had become solemn rather than her perpetually cheerful self.

'Nothing,' Kylie responded, trying to appear unruffled.

Taylor paused warily. *Talk to me, please*, his green eyes pleaded as he gathered her into his arms. Kylie cowered in his embrace, dropping her head.

'Kylie, I want to date you. I'm not after a hit and run.'

'What does that mean?'

'I'm not after a one-night stand. I don't think of you as meat on a sheet. I realise we have not known each other long, but I have genuine feelings for you. This is not just a physical attraction or lust. I asked you to date me because I am attracted to you. I like you very much. I want to be with you, but ... I can see now that you are not ready. I was not meaning to rush you. We don't have to do anything.'

Kylie remained silent, unsure what to do.

'When we get home, we will just dial everything back, okay?'

Kylie gave him a single reluctant nod. Taylor kissed Kylie on her lips, concerned that she looked worried. The drive home in silence seemed excruciatingly slow. When they arrived, Taylor momentarily held Kylie's hand firmly before she left the vehicle.

'Let's talk upstairs.'

Taylor released her hand after kissing her knuckles again tenderly. Kylie hung her head, searching inside her handbag for her door keys. The moment they were inside, Taylor hugged Kylie in a warm tender embrace.

'I'm so sorry, Kylie. I did not mean to put pressure on you.' His tone was measured and sincere.

'We are good,' she said, feeling stupid and naïve.

'No, we are not, Kylie! I've upset you and I did not mean to. I got carried away ... you felt so good.'

'It's my fault, too.'

'I want you to tell me exactly how you feel, Kylie.'

'I felt a strong connection. In the surf, there was a longing inside my chest.'

Her throat had constricted. She looked skittish.

'Okay ... so, are you frightened?'

'Maybe conflicted? I want to kiss you and taste you again.'

'Okay, I'd like that too.'

Hayley, on hearing their voices, began scratching frantically at the laundry door.

'We will let Hayley in and give her some attention. Then, you can tell me how you would like to progress. The message I am getting is – slower!'

Kylie remained stationary while Taylor opened the door. Hayley raced in like a furry bullet.

'Did you miss us, cheeky chops?' Kylie asked.

Hayley stood up on her short hind legs for a pat, with two tiny front paws just reaching to below Kylie's knees. Hayley's tail wagged excitedly before she dashed off to retrieve her ball. Taylor lowered his solid frame to the floor. Instantly, Hayley climbed into his lap for a pat. Hayley raced to retrieve her ball before returning it into his lap.

'My turn, is it?'

Taylor rolled the ball about six metres along the hallway, watching the coordinated rapid pace of the tiny legs in pursuit.

After a brief game, Hayley curled up onto her small bed. Taylor grabbed Kylie's hand, pulling her into a hug, hoping for another chat.

'I just love holding you, Kylie. I loved what you were doing to me. I got too carried away. Come and lie down with me.'

'I might just shower, change and put dry clothes on first.'

'Okay.'

'Give me five minutes.'

'Sounds good.'

Kylie came into his room. She looked refreshed but resisted making eye contact. Taylor lay on his bed with Kylie curled up in his arms.

'Heidi, my fiancée, was my only other relationship. She was my world. When you touch me, the feelings you generate within me are intense. I'm sorry that I did not manage them well.'

'It's okay, Taylor.'

'Talk to me, sweetheart.'

'I'm not sure what to say.'

Taylor rolled over facing her, studying Kylie's turbulent expressions with interest.

'I'm frazzled.' Kylie took a few deep breaths, unsure what to do or say. 'You've done nothing wrong, Taylor. I'm baulking, that's all.'

'Baulking? Why? I thought you were right into me when we were in the surf.'

'I was ... I am.'

'So, what's changed? What are you thinking?'

'I'm wondering about a few things.'

'Like?'

Kylie dropped her head, attempting to hide her face in her long hair. She took a deep breath before continuing. Looking at her hands, Kylie said, 'Like needing to make a doctor's appointment to get a prescription for the pill.'

'Okay. That sounds sensible. How else are you feeling?' Taylor sensed Kylie's reticence.

'I was enjoying your bare chest on mine. It felt really good when you were rubbing my back. I did not want to unlock from you.'

'Me neither. So, you would like to get contraceptives, but what we were doing was not too much for you. Is that right?'

'Other than the condoms box I got for Timmy, I have nothing here. I liked what you were doing, but I have no control.'

'No control over what we are doing, or how you feel?'

'I can't control how I feel. I cannot stop the sensations

buzzing inside me, and I don't want to get pregnant.'

'Okay. Are you happy just to have a cuddle and kiss here?'

'Yes,' Kylie responded timidly.

'I will try to be less stimulating.'

'I enjoyed it a lot. When you were running your hands along my back, it was like being set on fire and being unable to extinguish the flames. My body felt alive. I craved wanting to keep your bare chest against mine.'

'Well, you get your contraceptives, my lovely, and we can do as much of that as you like.'

'I cannot wait. I loved being so close to you and those long kisses.' Her toes curled at the memory.

'Me too. It is important that you understand, Kylie, that it would not be just sex for me. I'll want to keep you as mine forever.'

'Perfect.'

'Have you had many relationships, Kylie?'

'No.'

'None?'

'None this far.'

'You've never made love?'

'No.'

'That is why it feels so intense. Your natural urges are kicking in, and your libido is ignited. Your restlessness and the way you were melting into me had me totally aroused. I was worried that I had misinterpreted the urgency I was feeling.'

'I felt like I had no control over my body,' Kylie confessed, feeling exasperated.

'Clinging to me the way you did made me lose my control a bit too. I totally agree about you getting contraceptives. I would like to satisfy that desire we both have. If you need to go slower when you have the pill, we will do that too. I was afraid we were being impulsive and impatient.'

'We are being impulsive. You felt so good.'

Taylor found himself tented again. 'Well, we are going to have to restrain ourselves to kisses and cuddles, if we can. The way you make me feel is beyond a chemical and physical attraction. I feel a deep longing for you and your company.'

'Ditto. I never imagined anyone could have such an effect on me. The craving in my body was so intense. Even my nipples were hard and tingling. When I get those contraceptives, all the craving ... the urges ... the restlessness. I want to experience all those sensations again.'

'You're killing me here, Kylie,' Taylor moaned and laughed. 'I want that so much, too. You can have as much of that as you like when we are responsible. Did you want me to use condoms too?'

'Yes. The pill will take some time to kick in when I am able to get a script; I'm not sure when. All I know right now is that I will make that appointment tomorrow.' Gazing into Taylor's eyes, Kylie whispered, 'I know that I seem like a contradiction, but I want you.'

Taylor wondered how he was going to sleep!

Kylie raced out to use the internet on her phone. 'It takes a week if I start in the middle of my cycle, or it is effective immediately if I start after my period,' she read aloud.

'I will buy condoms tomorrow. That way we are both taking responsibility. We will continue using condoms until you have been on the pill and had your period. But I want to emphasise that I want you to determine when you are ready.'

'I know you are not in town long, but it would be good to spend this time before intimacy getting to know each other a little better. Let's use this time to quiz each other on any random topic we think of. What would you like to know?'

'Anything you want to tell me, really ... I know! How about you tell me what don't you like, or would change, about me, Kylie? Be honest,' Taylor said, trying to cool his attraction in their current circumstances.

Kylie replied, 'That's easy.'

Taylor looked up on alert. She had his full attention.

'I worry that your work in special forces puts you in danger. I worry whether, as my new partner, you will be safe.'

After worrying that Kylie was about to identify major character flaws, Taylor exhaled a sigh of relief. 'That is a hard commitment to make. All I can say to that is I will try my best, Kylie,' he said, delivering a kiss.

'I will miss you when you leave too, even though we have not known each other long.'

'Me too. I am really not looking forward to leaving town this time. I think I will try to organise two months' leave when I get back.'

'What would you change about me?' Kylie questioned.

'Oh, that's easy, too. What I would change is getting to know you better before intimacy. I am concerned that we have become so physically attracted to each other that we are talking about having sex before we really know each other. I would like to know more personal information about you while we are waiting for the contraceptives to work. I'd like to know what you like, what you don't like. I don't like this sense I have, that we are starting this relationship in the middle. I don't even know your middle or last names.'

'That's a fair point. Okay, I am Kylie Mae Black. I am twenty-six years old. I enjoy learning about angels, animal spirit guide messages, crystals and herbal medicine. I enjoy aromatherapy too. My favourite clothes have little flower designs.'

'It is interesting the way you talk about angels, like it is different to religion.'

'We get taught in nursing that there are four components to health: physical, psychological, social and spiritual.'

'So, when you say spiritual health, you are referring to your beliefs?'

'Yes. The angels, spirit guides and angel numbers are all an important part of my belief system. They are how the spirit world communicates with me. Now your turn.'

'Okay. Taylor James Robinson. I am twenty-eight years old. I enjoy being outdoors, hiking and jogging along natural bush tracks and rock climbing. I like wearing linen and cotton clothes in autumn colours like greens and light browns. I like citrus fragrances.'

'Those colours really suit you. I've noticed that your eyes change colour when you wear greens and blues. They become more vivid.'

'Okay. Tell me about one of the biggest mistakes you have made.'

'Probably my worse mistake was letting Jack stay at home longer than I should have. I still feel so guilty.'

'That was Jack's wish. Another big mistake.'

'Is there any reason you are asking me all these negative questions?'

'Yes, I am trying to cool my brakes while lying this close to you on a bed.'

'Okay, I get it. I made a very memorable mistake one time, after working with only eight hours between two shifts. My friend had an indoor spa a metre away from her laundry. I had two jobs I needed to do for her: put on a load of washing and top up some chlorine powder in the spa. So, really exhausted and not paying attention, I ended up putting the chlorine accidently in the washing machine, burning a hole in the load of clothes, and the spa ended up with a head on it like a beer when the washing powder accidently ended up in there. I multiplied my workload horrendously, having to throw out clothes and drain the spa. It was hideous.'

'Oh, that would have been the dizzy limit!'

'Yes, the spa only drained out three quarters of the water automatically. I had to remove the rest of the soapy water in buckets. What was your biggest mistake?'

'Like you said, it was probably going on a mission six months ago with Dad so vulnerable. Then jumping to conclusions about not being told I was adopted.'

'One goal you would like to fulfil?' Kylie asked, trying for a positive note.

'I would like to buy you a friendship ring as a sign that I am committed to a serious relationship with you. I would like our attraction for each other to develop into a deeper love. Your turn?'

'Oh, yes, I am interested in a long-term relationship with you too. I would like to learn more about you every day ... before the contraception cover cuts in, and we progress to the next level.' Kylie looked down momentarily before continuing. 'I am having difficulty at the moment distinguishing between love and lust with the intensity of the sensations you trigger. I had not anticipated this would happen. I had asked you back here, hoping to get you on board with letting Hayley and I live with Jack to help him. I had no idea that these heightened emotions I feel with your soft kisses were even possible.

In saying that, I have no regrets.'

'I am totally on board with all of that. Okay, another fun fact about you.' Taylor said, kissing her, running his tongue along her lower lip and teeth.

'I use crystals and colours to elevate my energy and mood. Your turn.'

'I like to jog or take a long walk to elevate my mood.'

'Then we need to keep those coping strategies happening while you're here. Using the usual stress coping mechanisms that work for you are more important at the moment. Let's walk around the zoo tomorrow before the hospital. Is that okay?'

'Yes, I'd love that. Okay, tell me about a funny event.'

'Well, since you have met Sally, I will tell you about us at uni together. Sally and I were picking our subjects for a semester. Sally pointed out that we already had compulsory subjects with two exams at the end of the semester, so she wanted us to pick a subject with no exams, just assignments. I wanted to do "pastoral care" for our third subject. At our residential school in the previous semester, students were talking about getting leeches and ticks on them, so Sally wasn't having a bar of that. Sally is so horrified of bugs and resistant that I had to clarify with her that the group bitten with leeches and ticks were biology students, and pastoral care was about religion!'

Taylor smiled.

'Now your funny event.'

'One Christmas during school holidays, my parents thought it would be fun to organise a pirate's treasure hunt. It was to entertain the children of their friends who lived on a farm. We bought little trinkets and treats for them to find. We got pirate hats, swords and a replica parrot to wear on their shoulders so the kids could feel like it was a real treasure hunt. We dressed the kids with a black patch over one of their eyes too. As we entered the property, we put a large bright bird on the mailbox, then hid treasures in their hay sheds, cattle yards and water tanks before we arrived at the house. All six of us piled in the car: the farmer's wife, their two children, my parents and me. With the kids suggesting the hiding places, the farmer's wife was driving us all around their large property. She was heading down to the mailbox where they could all see the huge bird. You couldn't miss it. As we got about a hundred yards from the mailbox, her husband came around the corner from the other direction. When he saw the colourful bird on the mailbox, he thought someone's pet had escaped. The farmer took off his shirt, and with it stretched out, he furtively approached the mailbox to catch the bird. We were screaming and laughing because he didn't know about the treasure hunt.'

Taylor smiled blissfully, mesmerised by the dimples appearing on Kylie's drop-dead gorgeous face.

'I know a question I wanted to ask you. What have you got against soap? There is no soap anywhere in this house.'

'That is because scientific research suggests that soap is alkaline and our skin is acidic. Soap kills all the normal germs called commensals that live on the skin. The commensals are the germs that importantly defend the body. The skin is one of the largest and most significant defence organs of the body. After using soap, a healthy person's skin takes about four hours to recover. A sick person's skin takes about twelve hours to recolonise with the commensals again.'

'That is news to me. I wondered why there was no soap at Dad's house, either.'

'We buy the washes that are pH balanced, because they have the correct acidity for his skin. Jack already has dry skin problems and an ulcer.'

'Well, I have learnt something new!' Taylor responded enthusiastically.

Chapter Fourteen
Sally scalded

*G*reg arrived at work for his evening shift to hear Sally's delighted giggle. She was so entertained that she could hardly contain her mirth to convey what had happened, without breaking into another laughing fit and pointing speechlessly at Jenny, the young English doctor.

'We just admitted a tomato farmer, Harry, after he was envenomated by a taipan,' Sally explained, struggling to continue. 'Dr Jenny told him that she had been in Australia for five months and had not even seen a snake. She was curious about how Harry had got bitten. Harry said he "just went to pick up a stake and the snake bit him". Jenny said, "Was it in your freezer?" She had such a look of horror on her face. She thought that we have so many dangerous creatures in Australia it is not even safe to open the fridge! She did not know what a tomato stake was.'

Greg's face lit up. Feeding Jenny's paranoia, he teased,

'You can't be too careful, Jenny, particularly when you are putting on boots.'

'Boots?'

'Yeah, shake them for spiders before you put your foot in.'

Sally giggled again nervously, shivering and cringing in sympathy with Jenny's grimace. She herself hated just thinking about disgusting creepy spiders.

'You're having me on!'

'No! Particularly if you leave your boots outside.'

'I thought you were teasing me.'

'I was a little, but spiders can hide in your boots.'

'Oh, okay. I'm never sure what to believe with you Aussies,' Jenny commented.

'Why's that?'

'When I first arrived in Australia, we hired a tour van. Some bastard in a caravan park told us to be careful of toads!'

Sally stared at Jenny, flabbergasted. 'What? Eating them?'

'No, the larrikin told us the toads could spit venom two metres,' Jenny elaborated. 'So, we were squealing and hopping everywhere, trying to get to the toilets and showers at night with the toads all crowded around the lights.'

At the image, Sally's melodic laughter erupted again. Jenny's face looked so comically pitiful that Greg too was grinning.

'That's funny! The Poms are the best value for a prank,' Greg conceded. 'Years ago, the Australian government tried to educate tourists on our venomous creatures. They put television advertisements on airplanes and in motels to inform the tourists to be mindful of sea wasps, thinking the "sea wasp" term was self-explanatory. The problem was they did not show the tourists what they looked like. So, when the tourists went to the beaches, they were looking in the air for the wasps but stepping on them in the water.'

'At home, we do not have all the biting and stinging creatures Australia has,' replied Jenny. 'In trying to learn antidotes, I'm getting a bit paranoid. I have been trying to learn all the envenomation protocols of everything from insects and spiders to stone fish and cone shells. There are so many venomous critters that I am intending to buy a text with pictures to have on hand. I will need pictures to remember what all those dodgy ants and creatures even look like.'

'It will probably be easier for you just to focus on what's in this neighbourhood, Jenny,' conceded Sally.

'Another thing to remember,' continued Greg, 'is that usually the snakes are fairly conservative with their venom. Unless they are threatened or nervous, they prefer to keep their venom to catch a feed.'

'I'm not sure that I am relieved,' Jenny replied, rubbing the goose flesh on her arms.

Sally laughed empathetically at the unsettled

expression on Jenny's face. Watching Sally's mouth corners twitching, Greg felt his usual stirring desire.

'Please help us!'

Blood was visibly dripping onto the floor from bay two where a young resident doctor was struggling to put in an arterial line. Sally rushed over to press on the artery and restore young Dr John's glasses back onto his nose.

'I'm sorry for the mess, girls', John apologised. 'When I went to thread the plastic cannula over the guide wire, these annoying glasses slid down my nose and everything went out of focus. Thanks, Sally.'

'You're welcome.'

'My new glasses need the frames tightened.'

Conscious of the blood still dripping off the blue absorbent pads onto the floor, John looked down, shaking his head, annoyed with himself. John knew, from his limited experience, that critically ill patients tended to be anaemic. He therefore felt incredibly guilty about wasted blood onto the floor.

'I am so sorry.'

'I'm sorry I couldn't help you, John,' Alice said defensively. 'She just woke up when you put the cannula in, so I had to protect her airway.' Alice stood at the head of the patient's bed, guarding the breathing tube of her ventilated patient. 'I had given a bolus of fentanyl and midazolam for pain relief and increased the infusions for the procedure, but she woke up abruptly at the wrong time.'

With the arterial line connected and secured with

a suture, Sally began wiping the bed rails and the bloodstained floor. John finished cleaning up the trolley after the procedure before ripping off his mask in frustration. With his gloves still on, John began wetting a disposable washer to clean the bed rail.

'Oh, you gotta be a grub before you can be a butterfly,' Sally said, lightening the atmosphere.

'Mate!' teased Greg from the next bay, looking at the mess. 'You're definitely still larva.'

Greg elbowed John in jest before opening a new stitch cutter in order to use the handle to tighten the loose screw visible on the left side of John's glasses. After putting them back on, Greg removed them a second time from John's nose again to slightly adjust the nose levers.

'That looks a bit better. Do they feel tighter?'

'Yes, thank you, Greg.'

John dropped and shook his head side to side, with no movement from the glasses.

'Much better!' John patted Greg on the shoulder.

Greg leant down to retrieve the dangerous drug cabinet key hanging from a red lanyard around Sally's neck. With Sally wearing her navy V-neck ICU scrubs and at floor level, Greg diverted his eyes away from the glimpse of Sally's cleavage on display. He was finding himself becoming more smitten every day. Greg's soft brown eyes looked admiringly into Sally's wide blue ones before turning to count the dangerous drugs before the staff from the previous shift left. He'd silently winked to be discreet so as not to alert any of their colleagues of their growing relationship.

*

The next day, Sally greeted Alice for their next shift together. Sally was watching Alice checking her emails on the computer.

'How are you today, Alice?'

As Alice turned on the desk chair, her arm accidently knocked her boiling hot coffee over, splashing Sally's right side, lap and thighs. Sally squealed in pain before rushing for the tap to cool the boiling hot water scalding her skin. With her skin still burning, Sally rushed into the patient bathroom, drenching her uniform, along with her watch and the items in her pocket under the cold shower water.

'Oh, Sally! God, I'm so clumsy,' Alice said, apologising profusely. 'I was focused on the email about my training due next week. I completely forgot about the coffee I'd just poured when I spun around.'

Panicked by excruciating pain, Sally frantically splashed cold water from the patient's shower onto her groin as she stripped off her scrubs top. She closed the patient bathroom door to kick off her scrubs pants and shoes.

'I'll get you some theatre scrubs, Sally,' Greg heard Alice call out. Standing at his ventilated patient's bedside, Greg looked over wondering what had happened.

'Jenny, can you go to the patient bathroom and check on Sally, please?' Alice asked the ICU doctor.

'What's happened?'

'I accidently knocked my hot coffee onto her when I spun around on my desk chair to say hello.'

'We keep a tube of SSD cream for burns in the fridge,' suggested Greg.

Feeling helpless, Greg asked the nurse at the next bay to keep an eye on his patient while he whispered to Jenny.

'I realise I am breaching confidentiality here, but can I just mention that Sally is diabetic? It's not common knowledge,' Greg whispered. 'I am just telling you in case Sally needs antibiotics.'

Greg retrieved the burns cream, sterile gloves and some sterile gauze for the doctor before returning to his patient's bed area. On seeing the day team leader return from her ward emergency, Greg called her over.

'You may need to call in another nurse for the night shift,' he suggested. 'Sally just got scalded with hot coffee. She's in the patient's bathroom. I'm not sure if she needs to go to the Emergency Department.'

'Oh, hell! That's terrible! Is she okay?'

'I'm not sure. It sounded like she's in considerable pain.'

'Alice, can you complete the incident report, please? We will need to replace Sally's shifts for at least a week,' Dr Jenny mentioned, discussing the scald with the team leader.

After finishing his handover to the oncoming shift nurse, Greg insisted on giving Sally a lift home.

'But I've got my car here,' protested Sally.

'I can get someone to pick me up from your place if you want. Or we can leave my car here and I'll drive your car home if you prefer. Or I can leave your car here overnight and ask security here to keep an eye on it.'

'Okay,' replied Sally, feeling defeated and shocked. 'You will need your car, so if you drop me home, I'll get my car tomorrow,' Sally replied.

On their way to Sally's house, Greg asked tentatively. 'Can I stay with you tonight, please? I realise this has been yet another blow for you. I just need to know that you are okay.'

'Thank you.' Sally dropped her head and swallowed, attempting to fight back her tears.

Greg put his car in Sally's lock-up garage before moving around to the other side to help her get out. Concerned at the brave front Sally was erecting, he stepped closer to give her small shoulders a hug.

'You're looking a bit pale and pasty,' Greg said, applying a gentle kiss to her forehead.

He stooped to collect Sally's wet clothes and handbag out of his back seat.

'Come on, let's get you settled,' Greg gently encouraged.

Leaving the wet clothes and her handbag on the kitchen table, Sally pointed the way into her bedroom. Greg slowly helped Sally remove the theatre scrubs and dressed her into a nightie.

'Ouch, that looks really sore, Sally.'

Greg looked concerned at the inflamed right side of her abdomen and thighs. Keeping her nightie down, he said, 'Your knickers are saturated. We'll take these off. Do you want me to get another pair for you to step into, or are you happy to keep them off? There are large blisters forming everywhere.'

'I'll just keep them off for the moment,' Sally said, lying down. 'These burns are really painful.'

'I'm going to get a washer from the bathroom to preserve your privacy. Then if that's okay, I'd like to put some more SSD cream and dressings over these burns. A lot of the cream has come off on your clothes as you got in and out of the car. The non-stick dressings have also migrated as you walked to the carpark too.'

'Okay,' Sally grimaced. 'I'm sorry to be a bother.'

'It's no trouble. Let's get you comfortable. Do you have any pain?'

'Yes, I'm a bit worried about anything touching my skin.'

Sally's hands were elevated protectively guarding the burned skin area.

'I brought some extra dressings, spatulas, burns cream and sterile gloves back here. So just have a rest while I gently apply more antibiotic cream,' Greg instructed.

Greg looked up as Sally's mortified face began turning as crimson as her burns. More hot tears burned her eyes before streaming down her cheeks.

'I'll try to give you as much privacy as I can, Sally, I

promise. I'll just put a washer over your groin and do the dressing so you don't get any infections, then you can rest.'

Greg covered the burns with sterile gauze squares lathered with the Silver Sulphurdiazine cream. 'If any of these blisters get too big and tender, I will pop them with the sterile needles Jenny included with the dressings.'

'Thank you. I am just really hot and tender everywhere at present.'

Sally started to tear up again.

'Under the washer,' Greg asked warily, 'did Jenny check there?'

'No, it's okay. I can't feel any burns there.' Sally blushed profusely, unsure where to look.

'Are you sure?' Greg persisted. 'As you know, a bacteria-prone area on a diabetic can be susceptible to a high risk of infection.'

'I can't feel any pain there at all.'

Greg backed off, ambivalent about stressing Sally further. Taking off his gloves, Greg tenderly kissed Sally's forehead. She looked gutted and overwrought. Sally's blue eyes spilled tears again as she began quietly sobbing and sniffling. Taking a deep breath, Sally dabbed at her sodden eyes with a tissue.

'I'll be okay. You go and have a shower if you want. The towels are under the sink in the vanity. Would you want a drink or anything?' Sally offered.

'I'll take a shower and then get us both a drink if you like. Are you up for a chamomile tea?'

'That would be lovely. Thank you again. I should have had my fill of hot drinks today,' Sally half laughed at her hideous humour. 'Don't make it too hot, please, in case I'm clumsy.'

Greg grimaced sympathetically before heading for the shower. He re-entered the bedroom with his boxers on and a towel wrapped around his waist. 'When are you due for your insulin, honey? I know you've had some heavy-duty painkillers. I just want to help you manage your diabetes while you're sleepy. Our teamwork will get you through this challenge.'

'Six am. I usually eat an evening meal at six and have crackers and cheese at nine to stop low blood sugars happening overnight ... Oh, hell! I left my lunch in the fridge at work! Are you happy if we just put frozen dinners in the oven for our evening meal? I'll have to eat before the injection in the morning, too.'

'Is your insulin pen still in your handbag?'

'Yes, I have twelve units not due until 6 am.'

'Okay. I will just help you monitor everything while you're on the painkillers.'

'Thanks, that's no problem. I usually check my sugar level at 5.30 am and pm.'

'You have a rest, and I will wake you up for 5.30 then. I'll just put your wet uniform in the wash and wash my clothes too, so I have clean clothes dry for tomorrow. If I can't figure out your washing machine, I'll do them by hand. Thank God that was my last shift for a while. I'm glad I've got four days off now to support you through this trial. I wanted to spend more time with you anyway, if that's okay?'

Sally nods, beyond exasperated at this latest setback.

'I'll need to go home to get some more clothes in the morning, though.'

'I'm miserable company at the moment, I'm afraid,' Sally commiserated.

'That's totally understandable! You've displayed more grace with Alice than I would have been capable of, under the circumstances.'

Chapter Fifteen
Embarrassed Sally

*G*eg retrieved Sally's saturated knickers and the theatre garb before heading off to find the laundry. When he returned, Greg was relieved to find Sally asleep. She was sleeping on her side with a hand tucked under her left cheek and a tear-streaked face. He set his phone alarm for 5.30 pm before settling on the bed beside her.

Fatigued by his busy twelve-hour day shift, Greg dosed off briefly. He awoke abruptly to the sound of Sally sniffling. The sound of her muffled sobbing crushed him, as though these ongoing dramas were cracking her veneer. Rather than being refreshed from her sleep, she was distraught.

'Oh, honey,' Greg soothed. 'Are you sore again?'

Sally nodded affirmatively, looking helpless.

Greg looked over at the digital clock on her timber

bedside table. 'You're due for more painkillers.'

'My skin feels so hot and burning. I'm really uncomfortable,' Sally reported, appearing agitated.

'Okay,' Greg calmly responded. 'Let's start with getting more tablets for you. How about I disinfect your bathtub, and we get you into a tepid salt bath?'

Sally nodded, blowing her nose before mopping her spilling tears with tissues.

'Here we go,' said Greg, offering two painkillers with a glass of water.

'I'm beyond frustrated!'

Greg scooted around to give Sally a careful shoulder hug. 'It was a silly accident. How about after the salt bath to soothe your skin, I will redo your dressings? Let's get you comfortable,' Greg coaxed.

'I'm sorry,' Sally replied, helplessly weeping.

'You're no bother. I like spending time with you. Naturally, I would prefer you to be able to enjoy our time together more.'

Sally rolled onto her side, facing Greg. 'You're very kind.'

'You're very worth it. Now, I'll run that tepid bath. Do you have coarse salt in the kitchen?'

'No, just the fine salt I use to crackle pork rind.'

'That'll do the job.'

Greg filled the bath halfway, then took the SSD cream out of the fridge to let it warm up to room temperature. In the bathroom, Greg left the light off. He gingerly removed the tubular netted bandages securing Sally's non-stick dressings. With permission, Greg slowly helped her remove her nightie and helped her settle into the bath.

'Is the water warm enough or do you need the ceiling heater on?'

'The water feels good. It's a good height, too; it comes right up to my waist. I don't need the heater, though. I feel really hot.'

'Okay, where will I find a fresh nightie?' Greg asked, keeping his back turned to leave the bathroom, affording Sally some privacy. He heard Sally splashing water with the clean washer.

'Third drawer down in the dressing table.'

'Do you want fresh knickers?'

'No ... I am worried now. I think the scalding coffee did burn my groin and splashed my right breast. That is where the pain is worst at the moment. I did not know to put cream there. Thank you for leaving the light off. This is so embarrassing.'

Sally was conscious of having her entire body naked in front of a work colleague.

'Don't be. I am here to help you. I care about you,' Greg replied, turning around, conscious to focus his dark eyes on her crimson face.

'This just feels beyond hideous,' Sally exclaimed, angrily. 'This is not how I wanted our relationship to start. You're not seeing me at my best.'

'You're very special to me, Sally,' Greg softly reassured

her. 'It breaks my heart seeing you have such a rough time lately. I'm not worried about doing any of this. I like helping you. I want you just to focus your energy on healing, rather than worrying about everything. Can you do that for me?'

Sally dropped her face into her hands, despairing of the humiliation ahead.

'Did you get any sleep?'

'Just a little. I kept reliving the scalding coffee splashing me only to wake myself up, startled.' Sally unconsciously curled her lips before proceeding. 'Now, I'm bloody *furious* with Alice rather than the usual irritation I feel towards her.'

'Would you like your hair washed?' Greg asked.

'No, I washed it before I went to work today. I will wait another day. Then we can wash it with a jug of warm water. I'm ready to get out now. Can you please grab me a clean towel?'

Keeping his eyes on her face, Greg shielded her with the towel, taking the opportunity of their proximity to deliver a quick peck on her forehead. Sally wrapped the towel around herself, securing a corner fold into her ample cleavage.

Back at her king size bed and wearing sterile gloves, Greg reapplied the antibiotic burns cream with sterile gauze. Acutely aware of Sally's humiliation, Greg decided distraction was needed.

'I could get some DVDs when I go home tomorrow.

What kind of movies do you like? Do you like chick flicks or have any favourite movie stars?'

'I don't really enjoy violent movies. I probably need humorous ones at the moment.'

'Good. Now we have a plan,' Greg enthused.

'I have been thinking about what you said when you asked to date me ...' Sally began.

'Yes, I would like to when these storms clear. I understand that it's a bit overwhelming for you to start a relationship like this after exams, being hospitalised and now burns, you poor thing.'

'I take my life a day at a time. It is what it is,' Sally said, determined to accept her predicament.

'Actually, you manage your diabetes really well for a shiftworker.' Looking into her reddened blue eyes, Greg fixed his honey brown eyes intently on her, as he softly explained his stance. 'Sally, I consider relationships to be a real-world experience, so I want you to be clear that I do not just want to be around you for the sunshine and fun times. Life is a complicated roller-coaster of challenging times and joy. You are just going through a rough spot at the moment. It won't last.'

'I worry that this is awful for you, like you are nursing 24/7.'

Greg scoffed, 'You're not hard work, Sally! I want to spend more time with you. And if anything changes, we can work it out.'

'Changes? What kind of changes?' Sally asked anxiously.

'Whatever changes happen, we can work things out together. Whether you go into education or want to work part-time, all I want is to share this journey with you. The destination is negotiable. We can take our time during the journey. Slow and cautious is fine. I'm not here to pressure you.'

'Have you had a partner with a chronic illness before?' Sally enquired.

'Not a partner. My mum has a chronic illness. That is why I texted her to say I was staying at a friend's and will catch up tomorrow.'

'What does your mum suffer with?'

'Mum has bipolar disorder. Dad and I love her very much. We are very fortunate that she trusts us to do what is best for her. We have to act promptly to get her medications changed sometimes when she swaps from the manic to depressive phase. We keep her condition managed well. If Mum is deteriorating, I call in sick for family leave because she is the priority.'

'That would make it harder to get out of the nursing role.'

'I love being her son. I don't see myself as being her nurse, or yours. Sure, I use the nursing skills I have learned, but I want to be your partner, Sally Price. I'll do what needs to be done. I will focus my attention on you rather than your illness. I don't want you to think I am here to score points or take advantage of your temporary vulnerability. I have been as honest with you as with the

155

other girls who asked me out, Sally. I told them I was smitten with someone else. That was even before the conference. I had recognised that I was beginning to care for you a lot.'

'You are very sincere and affectionate,' Sally observed.

'I do not want to hurt anyone by lying, or date anyone who would not have my attention. It would be cruel to make them feel rejected or devalued. So, I told them there was someone else special.'

'*Before* I agreed to date you?'

'I don't use women to satisfy urges. I enjoy your company, Sally Price!'

'Do you get hit on often?' she asked, her interest spiking at the news of competition.

'Occasionally, I get asked out by women. I'm not a player; I'm exclusive in relationships. While I tried in vain to be cautious of the dilemma of being attracted to someone I worked with, I could not resist your charms. You are inspiring, an amazing leader. You have loads of qualities I admire.'

'Don't forget bare-arsed,' Sally jested.

'Yeah, that, too, at the moment,' Greg laughed spontaneously.

'Do you find it awkward, with us both working some shifts together?'

'Seeing you is always a highlight in my day.'

'You don't worry about gossip at work?'

'No! We are adults, hopefully soon to be in a long-term

relationship. It's all legal. No one can do anything about it. However, I will be discreet. I will try to keep my attention off you and onto my patients at work.'

'And if something happens and we split up?'

'I would still treat you as a colleague and with respect. You have my word on that. I am not after a fling. I want to make you happy and keep you healthy. Our private lives will remain private. I would never disclose intimate details of our relationship, whether we are together or apart.'

'Aren't you scared?'

'I would probably say I am more committed to this relationship than scared. I found the more time I spent around you at work, the more keen I became. I've not been attracted to anyone else the way I am with you. The more I tried to resist the hazards of a work relationship, the more intense my feelings for you got. I went to the ICU social events and spent my time looking at the door, hoping you would show. I was asked out to a barbecue by another nurse, but I had to decline. It was like no one else quite measured up.'

'Oh,' Sally smiled, as her mood lifted with that news.

'Did I hurt you?' Greg froze, moving the gauze square, loaded with the SSD cream.

'No, I said "Oh" because you mentioned that someone else was chasing you.'

'I keep my eyes on the goal when I know what I want,' Greg clarified. 'Now, my lovely!'

'Hmmm?'

Greg hesitated. 'We need to check under that washer. I'm afraid it is going to be up close and personal.'

'Oh!' Sally instinctively inhaled, shielding her face in both hands as a mottled rash climbed up her neck. She dabbed her eyes with the tissues retrieved from the box on her varnished wooden bedside table. 'I am not a gracious patient, am I?'

Greg hesitantly suggested, 'We've got some burns cream on that lateral right breast now, but I need to put the burns cream down there too. I need to look first to see the source of the pain. Where can we get a torch for me and a mirror for you to see too?'

Horrified at the thought, Sally instantly gasped before burying her embarrassed face into her rough hands again.

'I'm sorry, Greg. It is not that I don't trust you. I just wonder if this nightmare can get any worse. It is like there are no boundaries here. I feel stark naked with a colleague. It feels bizarre!'

Greg launched over, planting a kiss on her forehead.

'Sally Price, you can do this! Where can I get a mirror and torch? My concern is the bacteria naturally present in this groin area has had no antibiotic cream on the scald since the accident.'

'Yes, you're right!' Sally hesitantly sighed, summoning up her courage. 'I'd put my big girl pants on – if I could.' Taking a deep breath, she added, 'Okay, the mirror is in the dressing table's top drawer. There's a torch in the top drawer in the kitchen near the benchtop stove.'

Greg returned to find Sally's head dropped in defeat. Trying to distract her mind away from her embarrassment, Sally began taking slow deep breaths through her pursed lips. Determined not be obstructive, Sally willingly abducted her knees away from her body as though she was having a pap smear, before Greg asked her to. She took more big breaths before exhaling forcefully.

'Okay, I see the problem. Can you see here? You have a huge blister on your right labia. Can you see it?' Greg pointed, validating the source of her pain.

'Yes, that's right where the severe burning pain is,' Sally reported, as new tears welled up in her puffy eyes.

'Let's put a folded towel under your bottom. I will puncture the blister with a needle to reduce the pain and tension in the skin.'

Greg looked up in surprise when Sally erupted in giggles.

'That's not the kind of prick I thought you had in mind.'

Greg looked up, smiling. 'You're naughty ... and courageous!'

'This ain't over yet, Mr Roberts! I intend to get my own turn one day at this "up close and personal" caper you got going on here.'

Greg's spirits were boosted, hearing Sally using humour to rally to the challenge. She had reverted to her preferred defence mechanisms of joking rather than cowering.

'And you will get your turn! Now, I want you to put the hand not holding the mirror on my left upper arm, so that you will automatically squeeze me if it hurts when I pierce this blister. Your skin down there is very inflamed and under a bit of tension, so I will put three holes in to let that blister drain.'

Gingerly, Greg winced before using the needle to nick the large taut blister, putting painful tension on her skin.

'Ooowh! I can feel a bit of pressure,' Sally grimaced, gasping and pursing her lips.

Her calloused fingers tightened on his shoulder, as the mirror in the other hand wobbled. The panic in her shaking voice warned Greg her composure was disintegrating. He stopped, uncertain how to proceed. Choosing optimism, he talked to Sally calmly.

'I have just punctured the skin, and the pressure build-up should dissipate soon. Now, the burns cream. Okay, almost all done! You've passed your trust building exercise for the day. I don't think I can take that test public, though,' Greg flirted.

Sally suddenly pursed her lips, grimacing in pain.

'Ooooh … ooooh … it's stinging a bit. That constant intense burning sensation is not as bad now, though. I'm sorry that I have been foggy and emotional. I will need time to get over this.'

'There is no rush. We are just spending time together

for now. It is important that I remember to let my parents know I will be here for a few days when I go home tomorrow. As long as Mum knows that I am fine, she'll be okay. Dad will ring if he is worried, and I can go straight over.'

Changing the subject, Greg again used distraction to take Sally's mind off the intimate procedure.

'Can I ask if you have had many relationships, Sally?'

'No. The one I had when I was twenty years old I thought had cured me for life.'

'What went wrong, can I ask?'

'He was immature. He told me I was filthy and boring.'

'That's terrible! What on earth could possibly justify any guy saying something as insulting as that?'

'I got thrush when my sugars became uncontrolled after starting shiftwork. Of course, being on contraceptives did not help the thrush either.'

'What a total tosser! It's better to be rid of garbage like that! Did he destroy your confidence?'

'Yes, a bit. He treated me abysmally. I felt discarded. I was determined that would be my last relationship. Then you came along.'

'When you permit someone access to your body, I feel the least they can do is treat you with respect. Even though I'm sure it was painful at the time, it is always therapeutic to be rid of a toxic relationship. I am sorry that was your first experience.' Greg smiled before continuing. 'My mum calls people like that "owner-operators", as though it is the politically correct term for "wankers". My mum is very intelligent. She loves watching live comedies. She comes out with hilarious terms like that from their punchlines.'

Sally laughed openly, amused at the thought of the older generation using that term.

'What happened in your previous relationships?' Sally easked.

'I got my heart broken several times, from being too naïve really, I suppose. I wrongly assumed my partners wanted an exclusive relationship when they actually wanted variety, apparently. I got hurt.'

'Oh, I've never heard a male report feeling used before.'

'Well, we mere males have feelings, too. I don't have that concept of a relationship or treat women like that, so I guess I was unprepared for being treated like that. I'm ashamed to say it happened twice before I woke up to myself.'

'That doesn't sound like it was your fault.'

'I learned from that experience that some women only consider relationships as short-term entertainment. I felt stupid afterwards. I learned that I am just one of those people who lead with their heart.'

'That's not a bad thing.'

'Well, it didn't feel great to feel like a discarded toy. Anyway, thank you for trusting me. I've ... um ... got another embarrassing question for you.'

Sally looked up, giving Greg her full attention. There

was a pregnant pause as she swallowed with effort, as though needing a moment to compose herself.

'How would you feel about me getting a jug of room temperature salty water ready for when you go to the loo? Now that we have pricked those blisters, we could pour saline over down there each time you void, to prevent infections.'

'Lordy! This is like being in ICU. There are no sacred sites!' Sally joked. 'Yes, it's a good idea, I'll grant you that.'

'And ...' Greg hesitated, 'I've got another idea to boost your courage. We could start a score chart.'

Greg grabbed a folder and sheet of paper from her study. He divided the page in half, labelling one side "Greg owes" and the other "Sally owes". On the "Sally owes" side, he wrote, "Greg: an up close and personal interrogation". On the "Greg" side, he wrote, "Sally still owes Greg the date promised for this Saturday night". Greg knew Sally enjoyed a game. He hoped using her natural coping mechanisms would make her feel less like a victim and more intent on having fun. Greg showed Sally the scoreboard.

'What do you reckon?'

'Good idea. We can start now!'

Taken aback, Greg innocently asked, 'Start what now?'

'Get 'em off, Roberts!' feisty Sally said, gesturing at his boxers with a smirk more consistent with her usual self-assured manner.

Greg couldn't help but laugh. His charismatic grin

radiated across his face and up to his eyes. As demanded, Greg dropped his boxers instantly. He theatrically took a bow, endeavouring to appear uninhibited.

'Much better!' Sally teased, with a triumphant cheer. 'That'll stop me getting performance anxiety on the loo. I'll have a room with a view.'

Sally reluctantly returned her eyes to his face.

'See! We are both exposed, and there is no shame,' Greg laughed. 'Unless you get visitors! But we are not done yet. I still need you to lie on your side so I can check at the back down there. I need to check from behind that the SSD cream is all over and no burned area is left uncovered.'

'You're stretchin' the friendship, Roberts,' Sally said, rolling over. As she lifted her leg, Greg placed a folded over pillow under her uppermost foot to keep her legs apart.

Greg put on fresh sterile gloves. 'Sorry, but it is necessary.' Greg winced ruefully. 'Jenny has given you a script for antibiotics in case you need them. She put the script in the bag while I packed the dressings and gloves. Do you have a thermometer here? Jenny wants me to check your temperature daily.'

'Yes, in the first aid kit in the study. You can get it ... after you've finished here.'

Greg looked up curiously.

'I mean, afterwards ... so I can check out the back view,' Sally added, cheekily. 'You're not getting away with anything, mister! 'By the time I've finished with you, you will have no sacred sites left either.'

Greg grinned, delighted the game was on. 'Oooh! Now the sassy Sally is coming out, a new personality trait!'

'You bet! It's game on!'

'Well, Sassy Sally, that big blister on the labia seems to be the worst of it today.'

Greg relaxed, preferring Sally's bantering to her withering from embarrassment.

'When I moved just then, more fluid gushed out of that blister. It feels much better.'

'Oh well, I've earned a slow kiss for that move, then, payable when you are up for it.'

Sally leant forward, pulling Greg's arm to bring him in closer.

'Good job, nurse,' she complimented, giving him a tender kiss on the lips. 'Now you can get the thermometer. I needed you to wait until I turned back over so I didn't miss out on your back view.'

Her eyes lowered, she blatantly sneaked another peek at his broad shoulders tapering off to narrow hips and his sculpted leg and butt muscles as he moved.

'It's a pretty amazing view so far.'

In response, Greg unashamedly did a pirouette at the doorway with his dangly bits flopping up and down.

'Tart!' Sally giggled.

'You're welcome!'

Entirely naked, Greg dashed off to retrieve the thermometer and glucose monitoring machine.

'Your temperature is normal, and your blood sugar is 6.2 mmol/L.'

'Great!'

'Don't worry, Sally. Even though this experience has been obviously daunting for you, our relationship will not be starting with your groin.'

'I don't know what to say to that. You were great. You kept me from stressing about this intimate body contact.'

'You say, "Great buns, Greg!"' he replied, slapping his own butt in jest.

'Okay ... great package, Greg!' Sally giggled, feeling strangely captivated by his naked body.

Greg's face lit up in amusement. When the compliment caused Greg to harden again, the effect could not be concealed. 'See what effect you are having on me, Sally Price?'

Sally boldly looked down with widening eyes. Greg felt those beautiful, deep blue eyes following him everywhere, distracting her focus off her pain.

'Good,' she scoffed.

'Oooh, so we are playing naughty nurse now, are we?'

'I wish I could,' Sally replied candidly.

'Plenty of time,' he flirted, smiling. 'At least at work, I can hide behind a gown.'

'I like your body,' Sally admitted.

'Ditto! You are beautiful, Sally, inside and out.'

'Well, I'd say that's an informed opinion. You have pretty well checked everything out!' Sally pouted before gazing again at the rippled muscles of his athletic body.

'You're an adorable package, Sally Price. But I will need to soak some small scissors in alcohol to clip the hair down there tomorrow, please.'

'There is a small pair of scissors in the dressing table drawer over there. The metho is in the laundry cupboards,' Sally responded, less apprehensively.

Changing the subject again, Greg questioned, 'It must have been hard injecting yourself as a child. At what age did your parents start letting you do the injections?'

'Twelve. I only got to double check the doses before that until my twelfth birthday.'

'You are brave, Sally Price! I don't know if I could inject myself, even now.'

'It does not feel at all a natural thing to do. Self-injecting feels like self-mutilating. Stabbing yourself with needles all the time and being restricted to chips and nuts at parties did not make for harmonious teenage years with my parents, let me tell you! When you are a child, it feels like you are being punished. As a teenager, I sabotaged my parents' efforts to keep my sugar levels stable. I drank ordinary soft drink, ate lollies and lied about taking my insulin.'

'Oh, what did they do?'

'They patiently explained to me that diabetes affected small vessels in the kidneys, eyes and peripheries, trying to make me comply, or worry about kidney failure and going blind if I didn't. Instead, I was rebellious and just got cranky at them.'

'At that age, I suppose it would be normal to want to blend in with your peers. As you know, teenage rebellion is a normal developmental milestone. At that age, you're supposed to separate your identity from your parents'.'

'If I had listened to my parents, I would probably still have friends. Instead, I made myself sick and accidentally peed on my friend's fabric lounge after drinking alcohol. My rebellion compromised my friendships and led to another shameful hospital admission.'

'You learned from your mistakes, though.'

'Yeah, the hard way! We had loads of fights when Mum and Dad tried to stop me having any money to prevent me buying alcohol or lollies. I was lucky when insulin patches were invented.'

'So, is that why you refused to let the hospital in Sydney notify your parents about your admission?'

'No, I just did not want to worry them. They have had a few health scares themselves recently. Mum had a mild stroke a few months ago, followed recently with a knee replacement. Just as Mum was recovering, Dad accidently tripped over a carelessly placed tool at a work site.'

'Blimey, your family need insurance!' Greg quipped. 'So, what turned your rebellious behaviours around?'

'The hospital psychologist. I was busy delivering my obnoxious teenage drama queen rant that had been well rehearsed after many arguments with my parents. I was going on about "why me" and "life isn't fair". He agreed with me saying, "You're right, life isn't fair. We all get different journeys. Some people get cancers and others get conditions that can be managed." It was a light bulb moment. While I still did not feel fortunate about having diabetes, I had not stopped to consider I could be blind or get renal failure. The penny dropped that I'd still be diabetic, but worse off.'

'I'm glad the right person was there, giving you the message you needed to hear at that crucial time.'

'As you saw in Sydney, I'm still a work in progress.'

'That was a simple mistake, Sally. None of us is perfect.'

'That Sydney conference experience was a case of "pride cometh before the fall".'

'Hey, it was a mistake!' Greg soothed, moving closer for a kiss.

'You were showing such an avid interest in me when I put on that exquisite dress in the shop. I didn't want to put you off, so I tried to hide my diabetes.'

'I'm sorry that you felt you had to hide your condition from me.'

'No one at work knows. I don't want people treating me differently. I like our team, which is why I want to get into education. I've learned a lot about diabetes from working too. I had a diabetic emergency one night, in a man whose skin was grossly swollen from nephrotic syndrome. I could not get blood when I pricked his fingers. The only sample I could get was all tissue fluid. The sugar level of the tissue fluid was 7.2 mmol/L, but I did not believe it because there was not any blood in the sample. He was combative and confused.'

'What did you do?'

'Well, my reasoning was that fluid is distributed under the influence of gravity. So, I pricked his ear lobe, considering that sample should have less tissue fluid contamination and contain the most blood. The reading was 1.8 mmol/L.'

'You're really clever, Sally. I would not have thought of doing that. I would have done an arterial stab. I imagine, with his skin swollen, he would have been difficult to get intravenous access in?'

'Yes, he was a nightmare. The low blood sugar left him so disorientated that he ripped out the only intravenous cannula in place. There was so much tissue fluid present under his skin that his veins were hard to find, so he had to have intramuscular glucagon. Eventually, we stitched a jugular vein cannula into his neck to get glucose into him. We needed security holding his head to prevent him bending his neck. It was touch and go for a while. There was so much fluid in his lungs the oxygen could not diffuse into his bloodstream. We had another security guard helping us keep oxygen on him, so that the nurses were free to deliver his cares.'

'That would have been challenging. No wonder the younger inexperienced doctors all report they are glad doing their ward medical emergency team calls with you. They comment about valuing your experience and your terrific problem-solving skills. You will be a brilliant resource as an educator. I've been qualified for eight years, and I'm still learning heaps from you. You are really clever, Sally. You motivate us all to be better nurses.'

'You sometimes just get more experienced with the years you work.'

'Why did you think your being a diabetic would turn me off?'

'I didn't want to be a high maintenance chick.'

'Well, let me tell you honestly how glad I am that you are coming around to the prospect of us becoming a couple.'

'I think we will just have to be cautious about distracting each other at work, though.'

'And,' Greg pointed at her accusingly, 'I shall have to wear a gown whenever you are around, Sally Price. You are one hell of a distraction.'

Sally giggled in delight. She brought her hand up self-consciously, covering her mouth to hide her glee.

'Well, it's good you're attracted.'

'You have given me novel experiences that I have never had before.'

'Like?'

'Tenting my trousers while catching maggots after you sprayed your perfume on my mask.'

Sally snorted as her abrupt laughter erupted again.

'You crack me up, Roberts! You are therapeutic for me. You stop me taking life too seriously.'

'You practically bust my trousers!' he accused.

Sally folded her hands over her face as her shoulders shook with her melodic chuckles.

'Now it will only get harder!' Then Greg laughed, realising his *faux pas*. 'I wasn't meaning *physically* harder. I meant I am going to have to be conscious of not staring at you at work. I will have to hide my attraction to you.'

'I love your way of taking my mind off my problems. You are hilarious.'

Holding her hand at a distance to prevent hurting Sally's burnt skin, they both shared the same bed. In the morning after Sally had eaten her breakfast, injected her insulin, bathed and had her dressings done, Greg headed home to grab some clothes and DVDs.

'Are you okay if I ask Dad to take me to the hospital so I can drive your car back here?'

'Oh, that would be terrific. Thanks.'

'Will it be okay if Mum and Dad want to meet you? You could stay in bed with the covers up.'

'If you like.' Sally smiled, processing his request as yet another sign of Greg's commitment to her.

'I don't want you to be a secret. I will tell them we work together and got closer at the conference. I will tidy up this room and the other side of your bed. I can put my bag in the spare room if they do come back here. Does that sound reasonable?'

'I wish I could dress properly to meet them.'

'They might want to just say a quick hello. I will put

your brunch coat beside your bed in case you need to get up for the loo. That way you won't worry about not being able to wear knickers. Oh! I better hide our score card too,' Greg said, grinning, as he placed it inside her cupboard.

'I think my brunch coat is still hanging on the bathroom door.'

'Okay, I'll get it. I will tell them you are on painkillers and not well at the moment, so they don't stay long.'

'Maybe you should clarify with them that it is early days with us, so they don't put pressure on our relationship.'

'Will do.'

Greg placed more painkillers and water beside her bed for while he was away. Sally watched, keenly interested, as Greg dressed back into his work clothes.

'The front door key is the green-edged one, and that key there is for the car. Thanks, Greg.'

Finally, he bent lower to give her a tender kiss on the lips. 'Back soon.'

Chapter Sixteen
Meeting Greg's parents

*A*t home again, Greg greeted his parents. 'Dad, would you mind doing do me a favour? I need to get Sally's car out of the hospital car park and back to her place.' Greg leant in to give his mum, Lilly, a kiss on the cheek, placing a hand on her shoulder.

'Sally?' Gordon and Lilly Roberts both echoed.

Lilly brushed her shoulder-length, layered, dark brown hair out of her eyes.

'Who's Sally?' she asked, her vivid green eyes following Greg with renewed interest.

'The girl I went with to the conference in Sydney. Sally is going to be off work for about a week. I'm just home to get some clothes and DVDs.'

'She's your friend with the burns?'

'Yes, Dad. There was an accident at work.'

Greg went to his room, packing three uniforms, shorts,

T-shirts, pyjamas, toiletries and his electric razor, trying to think what else he needed. Greg found both his parents hovering in the doorway.

'Sounds serious, son. How did it happen?'

'One of the nurses was sitting at a computer reading her emails. When she spun around on her chair, her arm knocked over a boiling coffee not long out of the urn. The hot coffee scalded Sally badly.'

Greg continued folding clothes and putting them into his duffel bag.

'Is Sally your girlfriend?' his mum asked curiously.

'It's all new, Mum. We had a lot of fun shopping together in Sydney. We spent loads of time together and enjoyed each other's company at the conference. We danced together on the gala night and walked around the zoo on another afternoon. I had asked Sally if she would date me. Sally had agreed that we would see each other this weekend and more on our days off. Now this has happened before we could even go out on our first proper date.'

'So, Sally's a nurse then?'

'Yeah.'

'From the hospital?'

'Yeah.'

'And you work together?'

'Sometimes.'

'Can we meet her?'

'She's probably not feeling too good at the moment. Sally is on painkillers, so she will be in bed. You could just say a quick hello if you like. Would that be okay? Come for a drive if you want. We can all go inside together and see if she is awake. If you keep the visit brief, Sally should be okay.'

'I'm excited to meet her,' his mum said eagerly.

'Me too,' his dad replied.

'Sally is genuinely lovely. You will both like her.'

'Let's take her some flowers.'

'Mum, that's a brilliant idea!' Greg kissed his mother enthusiastically on her forehead.

'What type of flowers does she like?'

'I know she wears rose fragrances. You just pick her something lovely, Mum. Sally will be grateful just to get her car back home. She feels very low. She's in so much pain she's not fit enough for a haircut right now, let alone company. So it'll be just a quick visit while she is feeling sore and hot.'

'Oh, the poor thing. Burns really hurt, don't they. How badly was she burned?'

'Sally was sitting close to the desk, so the boiling coffee got most of her right side.'

'Ouch, that would have hurt!'

'Yes.' Greg continued stuffing his duffel bag. 'Our ICU doctor gave her a week off to start with, and she will get another certificate from her own doctor if she needs it. Her skin is badly inflamed and blistered. Mum, could you help me pick some DVDs, please?'

'Sure, love.'

'Are you happy if I put in for the flowers? This accident has been such a shock. I did not even think of any romantic gestures like that.'

'Of course it is, honey. I hope Sally won't be frightened with us all rocking up there when she is already uncomfortable.'

'Sally is likely just to stay in her bedroom under the covers, Mum. As you can imagine, she's been a bit teary.'

When they arrived, Greg fumbled to find the right keys for the car and unit. 'Yesterday was the first time I have been here,' he explained to his parents.

Sally's eyes fluttered open at the noise of the squeaky front door opening. Greg put his duffel bag down inside the external doorway. As his parents entered, with his dad holding the floral arrangement securely, Greg shut the door behind them. Greg walked quietly towards Sally's bedroom door. He knocked lightly. Sally looked pale and drowsy, but she scooted upright on her pillows, trying to wake up and pay attention.

'Mum and Dad are here, hoping to say a quick hello,' Greg calmly announced.

'That's okay. I'd like to meet them,' Sally replied in a soft voice.

Greg signalled for his parents to come closer.

'Sally, this is my mum, Lilly, and my dad, Gordon. This is my lovely Sally.'

'Hello,' Sally responded, cautiously inching herself more upright.

'May we come in for a moment, please, Sally?' Lilly asked.

'Yes, certainly, I'm a bit underdressed, though,' Sally apologised, looking down to check that the front of her nightie was discreet.

'You're fine, love,' Lilly said.

Gordon passed Lilly the floral arrangement for Sally. Sally's eyes widened at the large bouquet.

'These are for you, Sally, from all of us.'

Sally gasped. 'Wow, they are so beautiful! Thank you very much. Now I'm feeling totally spoilt.'

Lilly brought them closer for Sally to smell before setting the flowers on the bedside table. Gordon smiled shyly, suspended awkwardly at the doorway.

'How are you feeling, love?' Lilly enquired.

'Not too bad. Still a bit sore.'

'From what Greg has told me, these burns hurt a lot.'

'Yes. It was all so sudden. I got such a shock when my skin instantly burned like the blazes.'

'I bet your parents are concerned about you, too.'

'I will tell them next week,' Sally replied.

'Next week?' Lilly looked from Sally to Greg in dismay.

'Sally's mother had a small stroke a few months ago, Mum,' Greg clarified. 'Sally does not want to worry her parents until they can see she is okay. We plan to visit them in a few days when Sally has less pain. They won't worry if they can see she is better.'

'Oh, I see.' Lilly nodded empathetically, satisfied with

the explanation.

'I was due to see them this Sunday. I'm hoping to be less sore. Most of the inflammation and swelling should be reduced by then.'

When Sally rubbed her face, appearing groggy, Lilly began to retreat from the room.

'We will let you rest, love,' Lilly said, gently patting Sally's hand in farewell.

'Thank you so much. I'm afraid I'm still a bit dozy from the painkillers.'

'You're fine,' Gordon said, as they withdrew after a brief wave.

'We will take your car home, Greg. You stay here,' Lilly suggested.

Greg put his arm around Lilly's generous girth, giving her a hug.

'Your mum wants to make you both a lamb casserole for tea,' Gordon said. 'That's what we were going to have, so we will make extra and bring it back after 4 pm, if that is okay?'

'You're the best, Mum!' Greg smiled approvingly.

Lilly also smiled, holding her son's hand affectionately.

'Thank you both. That will be better than Sally having frozen meals. No sugar in the sauce, though, Mum. Sally is diabetic.'

'Oh, the poor darling,' Lilly grimaced, looking back at the bedroom door concerned.

'That's a secret, Mum. Our work colleagues don't know. Sally does not like being treated differently when she is not sick.'

'I'm proud of you, son,' Gordon said. 'You've stepped up to life's challenges once again.'

'I've had the best role models, Dad.'

Lilly and Gordon left after another kiss and handshake for their son.

'Oh, God!' Sally exclaimed in frustration when Greg returned to the bedroom.

'What's the matter?' Greg looked around warily, seeing nothing amiss.

'I forgot to thank them for bringing my car back here.'

'That's okay. I will text them.'

'Dad, Sally is foggy headed from the pain meds. She is annoyed with herself that she forgot to thank you for returning the car.'

'Not a problem. Our pleasure to help out, however we can, xx.'

'xx ☺ see you after 4 pm.'

'Mum and Dad will be back after 4 pm. They are having a lamb casserole for tea and bringing some over for us.'

'Oh, how lovely! The apple didn't fall far from the tree,' Sally complimented. 'Thank you for bringing my car back, too.'

Greg moved closer, bending down in front of Sally's face, pointing to his cheek.

'Pay up, Sassy Sally.'

Sally lifted her arms, pulling Greg in for a tender kiss.

'Hmmm, paid in full,' he murmured.

Chapter Seventeen

Kylie's spiritual dimensions

*T*aylor and Kylie headed back to the hospital to check on Jack's progress as two kookaburras laughed loudly in the trees near the car park.

'Kookaburras are my animal spirit guides,' Kylie said, tracking the sound to search for them.

'What are they saying?'

'They are saying, "Laugh out loud. Don't stress", I think. Do you have any animals that you see constantly around you?'

'Magpies maybe? I've never thought about it really. When I was a child, there was a nest in the back yard.'

'That's interesting. They're a symbol of joy and love, the kind of childhood you have described.'

'You are into all this spiritual stuff, then?'

'Yes, the spiritual world is another dimension to our physical world that we can explore. You can believe events are astonishing coincidences or you can have fun interpreting the meanings behind them. Whether you believe in them or not, the messages are never designed to harm us. Usually our guardian angels, power animals or animal spirit guides give us messages to reassure us during times of change.'

'So, you are seeing good signs.'

'Yes, I am. It is not as absolute as science, though, and there are many aspects to consider. Every interpretation needs to reflect on the positive and negative aspects of the animal's nature. Like a spider can be a dream weaver or a red back spider could warn of a need for caution, like potential danger ahead. Most interactions are to give you more faith than fear. God wants us to be happy and live in joy.'

'I see you are a Christian. Do you go to church, Kylie?'

'Religion is man's way of reaching God, while communication with the angelic realm is God's way of reaching us.'

'Aaah, that explains your angel books and angel numbers.'

'Yes, they fascinate me. There is a whole angel hierarchy of archangels with dedicated roles. Archangel Michael, for example, can be called upon for protection, Archangel Raphael for healing and Archangel Raguel helps provide justice. There are ascended masters who have lived on earth to gain the human experience, like Jesus and Buddha. When Jesus is sending me messages, I get dry flaky skin in the middle of the palms of my hands or soles of my feet. There are beloved divinities like goddesses, elementals and our personal guardian angels who guide to ensure we are all well supported. They communicate in different ways, like through animal guides and angel numbers.'

'Numbers?' Taylor questioned as they entered the lift for the first floor.

'Yes. Zero is God. Seventy-two is God, too, as he has seventy-two names. Each number you see three times is a message. You will often see the same number on digital clocks or number plates. Sometimes you might stop at the lights and the car in front of you and in the next lane have the same numbers. The number fifty-five, for example, can indicate energy is changing or a situation is transforming.'

'Blimey, I've never looked. What do you see if your patients are going to die?'

'One time, a streetlight went off just as I approached it after my patient had died. It is all about being aware.'

'You fascinate me, Kylie. You are so positive about life's challenges. You always seem to have boundless energy.'

'The angels teach us to eat healthily and treat our bodies as temples by avoiding addictions like sugar. We have guides with us all the time to keep us safe and help us achieve our divine life missions.'

'What is your life mission, then?'

'To help others heal. At the moment, I am being encouraged to learn to use crystals.'

'Okay. So, what would my life mission be?'

'To protect us, maybe? I know that your work is confidential, so that would be just what I suspect.'

*

Jack was out of bed and mobilising slowly with a physiotherapist, who was encouraging him to correct his posture rather than stoop. The oxygen prongs in his nose were attached to a cylinder on the walking device. Taylor looked pleased, especially when Jack stopped in transit to look up with a smile.

'Well done, you!' Taylor encouraged. 'We will wait out the way, Dad.'

Jack looked down at Taylor's hands entwined in Kylie's. He looked back up to his son's face and smiled. His face lit up, pleased at this new development, as though understanding why Taylor looked more placid that day.

'Are you okay, Jack?' the physio questioned, as he remained stationary.

'Better than okay!' Jack replied excitedly. 'My son and my favourite nurse are here.'

'Jack is very lucid today, Taylor. He has noticed we are holding hands,' Kylie said, smiling.

'Good! Let's hope we can get him home.'

They both sat down to watch Jack shuffling along the corridor towards the patient gym. The loose hanging skin under his saggy jowls wobbled as he conversed with the physio.

'By the look of his progress, those assessments could be as early as next week. The way Jack is achieving, he could be transferred to the surgical ward for the skull fracture, or the medical ward for his chronic chest, very soon.'

'I'm starting to love kookaburras,' Taylor smiled. 'Every day, Dad is getting a little stronger. I like the way all these specialists, doctors, nurses, dieticians, pharmacists, radiologists and physios are coordinating his care. They're all helping him so much.'

'As they say, raindrops can move mountains. Don't be surprised if Jack is more forgetful, though, when he gets back. Look how far he has gone today! Jack is going to be so exhausted. He'll probably doze off again the moment he lands on the bed.'

'Dad has always been a fighter. When I was doing my schoolwork, he used to tell me to put in my best effort. He still does!'

'Have there been any updates from Annie, the social worker?'

'Yes, the investigator I hired to collaborate with her specialises in finding adopted children's biological parents. I asked the investigator to include Annie in their communication with me. They said my mother's maiden name was Maikie, but my father was recorded as "unknown". They are now reviewing marriage registries to find her married name. She then has to consent to meeting me.'

'How do you feel about that?'

'It's progress, I suppose, to know her maiden name. Though why my father is unknown raises more questions, doesn't it?'

'I am glad you are making progress.'

Their conversation terminated as Jack appeared in sight, slowly approaching his bed. Jack was so breathless from his exertion that he fell asleep immediately the physio settled him into his bed. Although they waited for an hour, Jack remained deeply asleep after his exertion.

'How about we check on your home and come back? Jack is not as breathless as he was, and he is no longer hyper alert and staying awake to struggle for each breath. If he was short of breath, he would be more restless. Instead, Jack is calm and showing the normal diminished physiological reserve that is common for his age. Jack sleeping so soundly is a good sign.'

With his left fingers entwined in Kylie's roughened hands and resting on his thigh, Taylor drove to Jack's house. Close to the back doorstep were five large magpies. Kylie and Taylor looked at each other, wondering if that was a sign.

'What do you make of that, honey?' Taylor asked, no longer believing this sight was an astonishing coincidence.

'Intriguing,' Kylie said. 'Those magpies are lingering for a reason. It seems like a message. The message seems to be a total of five.'

'Is that good or bad?'

'They are not attacking us to suggest danger. They are visiting.'

'Isn't that odd? I have never seen five here before ever.'

'You said you thought magpies were your spirit guide. I wonder if that means there are five in your immediate family or five will be visiting here? You, Jack and three others are alive. I wonder whether the five magpies indicate a family gathering.'

'The mystery deepens!'

'It does not seem to be a coincidence that this has happened when you are looking for family. I want you to keep an open mind and just observe this situation. My interpretation of this message is that it seems intended to reassure you that you are not about to experience loss. Let's go in the front door and watch them. I am keen to see how long they stay.'

Kylie stripped Jack's bed and changed his linen. She placed the dirty sheets and Jack's pyjamas into a bag to launder at her house. Taylor checked Jack's fridge diary and put the rubbish bin out on the kerb for collection the next day. Watching Taylor peering through the laundry window, Kylie's curiosity got the better of her. The five magpies remained loitering in the same location, pecking at the ground and looking around.

'What are you thinking, Taylor?'

'You will think I'm crazy if I tell you.'

'We are being open-minded and just observing, remember?'

'Saying this aloud, I feel like I've been whacked with the dumb stick. But now I don't want to leave until they do.'

'Jack will be asleep for a while, so you have plenty of time to watch them. The cleaning and maintenance services won't come if Jack's not here, so I am going to check the bathroom, toilet and fridge. Everything else looks tidy. I'll change the linen in your room, too. I noticed, when I went to retrieve Jack's hidden car keys, that your room looked a bit dusty.'

'I'll come and help you. Then we will return to our fine feathered friends and see what they are up to.'

When they returned, the birds had all gone.

'Well, we didn't think they would stay too long. Interesting, wasn't it?'

'Hmmm, I hardly know what to make of it.'

'Well, their message has certainly raised your awareness of the spirit world,' Kylie responded nonchalantly.

Chapter Eighteen
Meeting next of kin

*A*nnie dropped by, introducing herself to Jack, as Taylor was visiting him in the medical ward. By prior arrangement, the physiotherapist arrived a few minutes later.

'Jack, are you happy if I talk to Taylor while you are getting your strengthening exercises in the gym?'

'Yes, that's fine. My boy is the best. Taylor can answer anything you need.'

His actions had become more fluid and effortless each day. Jack now confidently stood onto the rollator.

'Can I just confirm with you, before we go, that you are happy to return home?'

'Yes, definitely! I'm working hard to get home,' Jack replied with determination.

'And you will be happy to go to a day care centre during the day, so that Kylie, or whoever is relieving her, can do their other patients' cares?'

'Yes, as long as most of my time is at home.'

'Okay then, Jack,' Annie said, shaking his hand. 'We will get that all sorted for next week. It's nice to meet you. I am pleased you are recovering so well. Just remember, though, that the "when" will be up to the doctor and your chest X-rays.'

'I'm a good patient,' Jack boasted.

Taylor smiled. 'I won't tell Annie about your stash of goodies, Dad!'

Jack smiled, momentarily struggling with his balance as he began mobilising. Taylor and Annie moved out to the waiting room for a confidential conversation.

'Taylor, I just wanted to touch base with you about the latest update on the adoption information.'

Taylor leant forward keenly, giving Annie his full attention.

'The information I have received today from the investigator is that your mother has carers. Her carers have requested that they would like to meet with you first, prior to them permitting you to meet your mother. Would you have any objection to that?'

'No, not at all. I would like their consent to my having a support person present when we meet. I have been fairly emotional since I found out about this adoption news. With Dad still recovering too, I feel the meeting will be smoother if I have a person to support me as well.'

'I will check and get back to you tomorrow. Can I meet

you out here about 1 pm?'

'Did they say why my mother wanted her family to meet me first?'

'I'm not certain that your mother is aware that you have applied to meet her family yet. From what I understood, you will be meeting her family first. As her carers, they want to fill you in on the background of your birth and about your mother's health.'

'Oh, okay. Did they say where they live? Will I need to travel far for this first meeting? I am reluctant to leave Dad or go too far out of town at the moment.'

'I am unsure where you will be meeting at this stage. Although you were born in Toowoomba, your mother moved after she married. I am not permitted to mention more than those details at this stage. My understanding is that the family members will explain more about her situation in person when they meet you.'

'Well, thank you! I am very grateful to you for facilitating this delicate process.'

Taylor's eyes instantly teared up as he processed this new psychologically taxing development.

Annie reassured Taylor in her soft articulate voice. 'It's been my pleasure. I will text you as soon as I know more. Can I ask if you have any other commitments beside Jack?'

'I am not expected to return to work for at least another fortnight. I have extended my family leave.'

'I am just wondering whether you might be happy for me to go ahead and arrange a meeting time. If you want,

I could try to arrange the meeting in the hospital gardens here, if you prefer. I am happy to be present, in case you need a debriefing afterwards. I realise the timing of this has not been ideal for you.'

'Yes, a meeting in the hospital grounds would be fine. It will be easier to bring my support person here, too. Or I might need a day's notice if I needed to book flights, assuming they live in Australia?'

'From my conversation with them, I got the impression that the family were happy to meet you here at the hospital. I am unsure if you would prefer the privacy of my office or to be out in the gazebo in the gardens.'

'I am always less stressed in nature, so the gardens would be my choice,' Taylor replied. 'However, I am also sensitive they may prefer more privacy. Go ahead and book an appointment where they prefer. I really appreciate your help, Annie.'

'I will book that appointment – that's no problem – and will text you with the time and place. I will also meet with you and your support person immediately beforehand, just to check you are not too anxious. I do appreciate how stressful all this uncertainty is for you.'

'Thank you. I will be nervous. Please reassure them that I had loving parents and am not angry about anything. I am just keen to meet them and understand the circumstances of my adoption. Naturally I would like to be introduced to them, as well as to meet my mother.'

'That's very thoughtful. I will do that, Taylor.'

Taylor walked back to Jack's bedside to wait. Jack returned slightly more breathless than usual after walking upstairs and extending his graduated gym work with the physiotherapist. Taylor smiled at the first sight of Jack returning. Kylie arrived not long afterward.

'How are you going today, Jack?' she greeted.

'Doing time with hard labour!' Jack puffed, winking at Kylie before diverting his gaze mischievously towards the physio. Feeling fatigued, Jack asked the physio to put him in his bed rather than in his recliner. Kylie and Taylor left shortly afterwards to allow Jack to rest before lunch, after which he again fell fast asleep.

'Are you able to get Thursday off by any chance, Kylie?' Taylor asked as they returned to the car park.

'I'll just text my supervisor and ask. What are we up to?'

'Annie has arranged a meeting with my biological mother's family for 10 am. I was hoping you could be with me, if that is at all possible.'

'I will do my best. If I cannot get the day off, I will be with you for the meeting between my appointments. I will reschedule and work later if I need to. I am glad that you are finally going to get some answers. I will try to get a rostered day off by swapping with one of the team. I will tell my supervisor there is a personal family matter I need time off to attend to. She is usually pretty flexible. We community nurses cover each other's patients when personal issues arise. If someone gives up their day off, I will pay them back.'

Kylie placed a comforting arm around Taylor's waist.

'Thank you, honey. I know you are incredibly busy. You just have this practical way of grounding me. I would really value your support. I am worried I could get anxious and scare them with a bad impression.'

'I really want to be present for you during this big moment in your life. I feel privileged that you are sharing it with me.'

'I feel so blessed that you came into our lives,' Taylor said, stopping to kiss Kylie's hands. 'Dad and I both value your assistance.'

When Taylor still looked nervous, Kylie suggested a jog when they get home.

'Pounding the pavement will use your normal coping mechanisms to de-stress. Your body will produce calming endorphins.'

'You're amazing! I don't know how we ever coped without you.'

Taylor tilted her chin upwards for a long kiss.

'You keep that up, buster, and we will need a shower together!'

'Hmmm, I'm up for that.'

Taylor smiled, aware Kylie was intentionally distracting him.

'Yes ... well ... you did promise me a rematch of our beach experience.'

'Hmmm, and you are ready, are you?'

Taylor became immersed in her sensuality and the scent of her sexy body.

'I hope so, this time. I don't want to disappoint you again. We will just progress slowly and see where the mood takes us, shall we?' Kylie whispered suggestively, her tongue following the contours of Taylor's ear lobe.

'You did not disappoint me last time,' Taylor clarified, kissing her around the neck and throat. 'I was the one getting carried away and being too hasty.'

'I did not want to stop you. But on the drive back from the beach, I just got nervous.'

'We will stop any time you need to. I'm glad we took the time to get to know each other more before getting intimate. The more I get to know you, the more love I feel for you, Kylie.'

'You are very special to me, too. I am pleased that everything is working out so far, as you had hoped.'

'This time, home feels like I'm getting three magical wishes,' Taylor joked, feeling more optimistic. 'Dad's better, I've found myself a lovely partner and now I am going to meet my biological family.'

'Remember what we said, though – no expectations of your biological family. We will just see what answers they can provide without judging them. You don't need to come away from that meeting with further obligations to meet them or your mother if you feel uncomfortable. We will just take one day at a time ... baby steps.'

Taylor hugged Kylie in a final sizzling embrace.

'See you at home.'

After they got home, neither Kylie nor Taylor made

it for a jog. Once they began pashing, their heightened emotions intensified to frantic kissing, until they both ended up under the shower together. Kylie lathered a citrusy bath lotion onto Taylor's skin, her touch becoming more urgent at the sight of his naked body. As Taylor placed a hand behind her head to part her lips with his tongue, Kylie clung longingly to him. In Kylie's bedroom, they both explored each other's naked bodies without restraint. She tasted his toothpaste and breathed in his masculinity, welcoming his erotic touch.

'Are you sure?' Taylor checked again before tearing open the condom packet with his teeth.

'Yes. I want total skin-to-skin contact.' Kylie looked flushed and eager. 'I need your chest pressed back against mine. I want our bodies locked together this time. I am more than ready.'

'We need to go steady,' Taylor said, kissing her cheeks with his stubbled jaw. Kylie squirmed as his expert touch ignited her passion. Her surrender was complete as he explored her eager body with undisguised lust.

Afterwards, as Taylor looked down at her naked body, Kylie snuggled into his athletic build. Taylor recognised how his feelings were growing more intense. He was fortunate to have found love again.

'I want to take you out to dinner to make this night more memorable for you,' Taylor sighed, stroking his hands rhythmically up and down Kylie's naked back. 'I don't want to remain lying in this bed with you. You are too tempting. I don't want to make you sore.'

'Hmmm ...'

'What do you say? Come out for a meal?'

'Hmmm, sure. I doubt anything could make this night more perfect,' Kylie said in peaceful bliss. 'I have loved being with you.'

'I love everything about you, sweetheart. I can't imagine going back to work, having to spend a single day without you.'

'We will do video calls when we can, like I do with Timmy.'

Kylie rolled her naked form on top of Taylor for another longing kiss and embrace. Her long hair surrounded his head like a drape, as her loving blue eyes searched his green ones. Her face was ablaze with a sexual flush.

'You made tonight very special for me.'

'You *are* very special to me. I hope how we feel about each other now remains for the rest of our lives together. I care a lot for you. I have taken none of this lightly.'

'Me neither. I feel very happy that you are here with me, and want me.'

'Let's go out to tea before you get my hormones raging again. We will have plenty of time to be together.'

'I can't wait.'

As they drove into the restaurant parking lot, their attention was drawn to a slim attractive young couple exiting their BMW sports car. As with their dress, mannerisms and their later menu choices, everything about the couple displayed wealth. Taylor and Kylie were seated opposite them across the aisle. Neither Taylor nor Kylie was surprised when the couple both ordered lobster meals costing over a hundred dollars each. In the opposing seats, sitting back-to-back with the young couple, were a young family with two young girls, all talking loudly. Taylor's face lit up with intrigue when Kylie got the giggles.

'That young family are so uninhibited, they are hilarious!' whispered Kylie, leaning close to Taylor's ear. Taylor began listening to the girls, who looked about nine and ten years old, back chatting their parents.

'After this treat,' warned their father, pointing to their odd menu choice of curly chips for entreé and pancakes for their main meal, 'I expect you to have your baths with no squabbles tonight.'

'Yes, Dad.'

'It's nit night,' warned their mother. 'You're both due for a nit shampoo and combing tonight before your baths, too.'

Kylie erupted in laughter again as the male yuppie's fork froze in transit to his mouth on overhearing their conversation. He pushed his plate into the centre of the table, as though his newly arrived lobster had suddenly lost his flavour. The couple stood up abruptly to leave. Kylie placed a hand over her face and tried to turn her head to concentrate on the wall to contain her amusement. As she looked over at Taylor, Kylie saw him biting his lips. His shoulders were shaking from restrained laughter.

Finding it becoming extremely difficult to control her entertainment, Kylie strategically slid out of the charcoal vinyl bench chairs to go to the loo. As she walked past the cashier, the young couple were paying their bill.

'How were the meals?' the waitress innocently asked, concerned the cooked lobster had not long been delivered to the table.

'We'll just say we ordered lobsters, not crabs,' replied the vexed male customer between tightly pursed lips.

One look at his sympathetic female partner and Kylie had to bolt fast for the toilet before she could no longer contain her amusement. Arriving back at the table, Kylie could not stop giggling to report the conversation back to Taylor. Kylie moved her drink over to the same side of the bench seat as him. One look at Taylor's handsome smile, white straight teeth and creased green eyes and Kylie could not help but think about how much she liked this new relaxed version.

'It is going to be horrendously difficult for me to leave you and Dad when I have to return to work,' Taylor said, looking with admiration at the bubbly Kylie.

'Yes, it will be challenging. We can video call every evening so that you can see Jack, too.'

'I will miss you both terribly,' Taylor sadly conceded.

'For me, absence is a small price to pay for someone risking their life for the benefit of all Australians. I will miss you very much, too, when you have to go back to work.'

'Long distance relationships are difficult,' Taylor

warned, looking sad. The mere thought of leaving both Jack and Kylie this time was daunting.

'Remember, we have loads of choices. Jack and I might be able to travel to you sometimes, for a week's holiday while you are away. I can ask my friend Sally to look after Hayley.'

'I would like that. There are several motels near the base,' Taylor said, looking hopeful.

'I guess when we cannot see each other on a screen, it will get more challenging. At least this time, when you leave town, we will both feel more secure that Jack is safe.'

'I'd like a photo of us both together to keep with me in my wallet or on my phone. I will look at you every day to help me when I miss you.'

'Yes, I would like some photos, too. I realise that when you had to reluctantly leave Jack for six months before, there could also have been longer painful separation stints.'

'Yes, I'm afraid so. I will keep you informed about dates. Unfortunately, I can only provide you with broad details of any work travel arrangements for security reasons.'

Kylie breathed deeply and sighed. 'I'm determined not to spend the rest of my time with you, grieving about missing you, before you even go,' Kylie said, with a longing kiss.

The tyranny of distance, Taylor contemplated, giving Kylie a heartfelt hug.

Chapter Nineteen

Taylor's growing family

*A*the hospital gazebo, Taylor and Kylie nervously waited with Annie for the arrival of Taylor's biological family. Annie had brought a jug of iced water, which was sweating on the tray around the five glasses. With his hands tensely locked in Kylie's, Taylor eyes were eagerly fixed on the concrete path walkway. He occasionally looked over at the cooing of pigeons or the melody of the chirping mynah birds, orchestrating enticing spring mating calls. Taylor's eyes wandered back to the concrete path periodically, before looking up at the hawks gliding on warm air currents above. He enjoyed the soothing effects of the natural sunshine on his legs and the gentle breeze blowing the tree limbs behind them. Trying not to squirm, Taylor inhaled deeply the subtle fragrant blossoms of the rose garden nearby. The hospital gardens were a clever combination of manicured hedges and native bottle brush trees; the latter around the periphery. Taylor felt a need to make memories of this life-changing day, so he could relive it forever.

A man in his late fifties with hair greying at his temples, wearing gold-framed tinted glasses, appeared walking along the path towards them. His tall, solid frame was dressed neatly in a beige, white and olive striped shirt and tan trousers. His shirt was tucked neatly into a darker tan belt around his portly waist. A younger tall man with shorter, dark brown hair, dressed in smart casual blue jeans and an ochre-coloured linen shirt with dark sunglasses wrapped snugly around his eyes, walked beside him. The younger guy chatted, nodding intermittently as he looked towards the older man as they strode purposefully along.

As the younger man approached the gazebo, he lifted his shades onto the top of his head. Taylor and the young man stared intensely at each other, gobsmacked. Taylor stood momentarily stunned before holding out his hand to greet them.

Shaking the younger man's hand firmly, he said, 'Greg, this is a surprise. How are you?'

Their stunned eyes remained locked in disbelief.

'I'm fine,' Greg said.

'Er ... this is my dad, Gordon. Dad, this is Taylor Robinson ... my ... err ... stepbrother, apparently ...'

'Pleased to meet you, Gordon,' Taylor said, shaking hands. 'This is Kylie, my partner, and I believe you have been communicating with Annie to set up this appointment.'

Annie shook both their hands, while Kylie greeted Greg with a smiling welcome that displayed their familiarity. Greg and Taylor then stood silently staring at each other, shocked.

'Oh, my goodness,' Kylie said, breaking the eerie silence. 'Small world, hey?' She smiled encouragingly at both parties, blatantly pleased about this new information.

'Do you all know each other?' Annie asked, confused, recognising the visible disbelief on Taylor's expressive face.

'We met recently in ICU,' Greg elaborated, 'when Taylor's father, Jack, was admitted.'

'And you had no idea?' Taylor asked, suspicious.

'I'm just as gobsmacked as you are, mate,' Greg explained, openly smiling. 'Taylor's dad was my patient in ICU a few weeks ago. That's how we first met. Then, a few days later, we ran into each other briefly again in the mall downtown, coincidently.'

'You said "stepbrother"?' Taylor queried.

'Yes, that was what we wanted to discuss with you today before you met my ... sorry, *our* mum.' Greg smiled self-consciously. 'I expect this will take us both some time to get used to.'

Gordon placed a supportive hand on Greg's shoulder before his son proceeded.

'Mum's name at the adoption agency would have been

Lillian Maikie. Mum suffers from bipolar disorder, a condition that often fluctuates between manic and depressive phases, with sometimes a combination of both phase symptoms present at the same time. In the manic phase, Mum gets really excited and exudes boundless energy, with her conversations racing from one topic to the next. In the depressive phase, she can feel very sad, hopeless, withdrawn and inactive. At times, Mum's disorder can be difficult to stabilise, because each phase often needs opposing medications or complex medical regimens to be prescribed. Sometimes, her bipolar disorder can be remarkably resistant to treatment. When Mum's mood changes to the manic phase, the anti-depressant medications prescribed for the depressive phase don't work. We asked Annie if we could meet with you first, because we wanted the opportunity to explain to you why your father's name is recorded as "unknown" on your birth certificate.'

'I see,' Taylor replied, leaning forward to pay attention.

Greg inhaled deeply before continuing.

'At seventeen years of age, my grandparents said Mum began talking rapidly. Her conversations were jumping from one topic to another. At the time, with no medical knowledge and undiagnosed, they dismissed the initial subtle signs of her disorder as senior exam nerves. As the condition progressed untreated, her conversations became obscure and illogical. At that stage, Mum had not been diagnosed with bipolar disorder, and these signs were dismissed as Mum not sleeping well and being awake all hours of the night. She began losing her ability to concentrate during her senior year and then progressed to a psychotic episode where she was totally detached from reality. Mum was still undiagnosed when she got pregnant. Mum remembers the later stages of her pregnancy and her parents needing to put her child up for adoption to look after her, but she has no idea who your father was.'

Greg focused on his hands as he spoke to avoid Taylor's intense scrutiny.

'Oh, I see,' Taylor whispered compassionately.

'So, unfortunately, we cannot give you any details there. Now, Dad and I are her carers. We wanted to meet with you first before we mentioned anything to Mum, as her mental health can be brittle. Her mood swings can fluctuate dramatically, to the point that stressful conditions can trigger relapses. We wanted to introduce ourselves first. We kind of ... well ... we need you to meet Mum without asking her questions.'

'Oh, I am sorry to hear that our mother is not well,' Taylor remarked sincerely. His eyes burned as they teared up in sympathy. 'What is my mother like?' he tentatively questioned.

'Mum is very happy most of the time. Our mum is loving, very caring, intelligent and witty, but fragile. Mum loves designing floral arrangements, cooking, watching movies. She especially loves comedians doing their routines on stage, live. We thought it might be best for her to meet you as my friend first, and then we could tell her afterwards. That way, we hope Mum might be less anxious about meeting her son for the first time, as she will have met you already.'

'I will follow your advice. You know what is best for her. I will only be in town for a few more weeks, though. When I leave town for work, I may not be back for a few months. I could catch up with her each time I come back to town if everything goes okay – and catch up with you both, of course? I would let you know in advance, if our meeting goes smoothly, when I will be in town, if that is what my ... *our* mother wants? Do I have any other siblings or relatives?'

'Yes, our mum's parents, your grandparents, are Paull and Violet Maikie. I will be happy to give you their Brisbane address once I have their permission. Does that sound okay?'

'Thanks, Greg.' Taylor was subconsciously squeezing Kylie's hand forcefully. 'I did not know I was adopted. Dad apparently told me when I was young, but I did not remember. I only found out when Dad was admitted to the Intensive Care Unit, when his doctors were talking about his Young's syndrome.'

'What's that?' Gordon interrupted.

'It displays three symptoms, potentially related to Dad's having mumps as a child: chronic chest infections, sinusitis and infertility. It was when I was on the internet looking up Young's syndrome that I discovered the infertility bit. Please don't say anything to Dad. There are drawers full of pictures at home with drawings of love hearts; Mum's, Dad's and my pictures are inside the hearts. Now, retrospectively, I finally understand what they were trying to tell me. Michelle, my adopted mother, was telling me about being born within her heart, not beneath it. I did not know anything about pregnancies as a child, of course, so I did not understand the context of adoption, or what they were trying to tell me. I actually did not remember being told about being adopted at all.'

'Gosh, that news would have come as quite a shock then!'

'Yes, my imagination was on overload. Fortunately, Kylie was there to ground me.'

'How do you feel now about having a stepbrother, Greg?' Kylie cautiously asked.

'I'm glad to have finally met Taylor. Dad is, too, I can tell.' Greg smiled.

'Yes, I am. I am glad that it sounds as though you had really lovely, responsible adoptive parents,' Gordon said.

Spontaneously, Greg impulsively gave Taylor a man hug.

'Who would have thought, when we met last week, all this would come about?'

'It feels absolutely crazy!' Taylor conceded.

'Dad, Taylor is a soldier.'

'Really?'

'Yes. Confidentially, I am in special forces, but that has to be kept a secret for security reasons. I am not permitted to talk about missions or anything like that.'

Greg looked over meaningfully at Gordon before suggesting a solution.

'I think it might be best to just tell Mum that you are a soldier. She may not be able to keep secrets with her illness.'

'Wow!' Taylor inhaled deeply. 'I cannot get over all that has happened so far this visit home.'

He smiled affectionately at Kylie.

Noticing her blush, Greg exclaimed, 'No way!'

'Yes way!' Taylor proudly announced, 'How did you fare?'

Greg's brown eyes creased with his wide smile.

'Sally has agreed to date me,' he declared.

Kylie grinned, clapping her hands excitedly. 'I'm delighted for you both,' she smiled. 'Good choice. Sally is amazing.'

'Yes, she is,' Gordon confirmed, nodding his approval.

'You look after her, Greg,' Kylie said, advocating for her absent friend.

'The more I see of Sally, the more smitten I become,' Greg acknowledged.

'You could not have picked a better girl,' Kylie echoed.

'Yes, Sally is terrific. She's becoming part of this growing family,' Gordon said cheerfully.

'Where is she today?'

'Mum is teaching Sally how to organise silk floral arrangements so that she was not alone while we are here. They both get along fabulously.'

'Sally would enjoy that.'

'So will Mum! Mum is glad to have more oestrogen in the house,' Greg laughed openly. 'If we are not careful, she will soon be planning grandchildren.'

Taylor laughed at his stepbrother's jest.

After an hour of peaceful dialogue, Greg said, 'Okay, we will see you again on the weekend at our house. I will text you the time and address, Taylor. You and Jack are invited, too, Kylie, if Jack is home by then. I was pleased, when I transferred an ICU patient to the medical ward the other day, to see how much Jack was improving. Jack did not look far off discharge. He was mobilising incredibly well.'

'Thank you for taking the time to answer my questions. You have a very caring manner, Greg. I was really glad to have already met you. I was feeling pretty nervous myself, almost to the point of panic. Your kindness and thoughtfulness have made this experience less stressful, even though I did not know we were related. Good to meet you too, Gordon!'

Taylor shook both hands firmly.

'Once we get Mum on board, I'm hoping you won't be a stranger,' Greg suggested.

'Me too,' said Gordon. 'Welcome to the family. I'm sure Lilly will be delighted to meet you and have you back in her life again. Lilly has always regretted that she was not well enough at the time to look after you. Nanna and Pop were severely stretched just trying to keep Lilly stabilised. They were exhausted from being up all night when Lilly did not sleep. Lilly cannot concentrate when manic, so they needed to keep any eye on her for her own safety. My grandparents felt that a newborn baby deserved more attention than they would have been able to give, under the circumstances.'

The group parted, after exchanging contact details.

'What does it feel like having a new brother?' Kylie enquired, as they strolled hand in hand back to the car park.

'Greg feels like one of those mates you meet that you feel you can trust immediately. Does that sound odd?'

'Not at all. Sally has had very few relationships. If she has chosen him, Greg must be worth it.'

'Greg took really professional care of Dad.'

'Sally did, too. I helped them both the first night when Jack was admitted. They were both genuinely caring. Nursing is not just a job to either of them; they are both the real deal.'

'You are all inspiring!'

'This has been a big week for you, Taylor.'

'Yeah, as they say, it's been a hell of a ride! Somehow, it seems as though the best may be yet to come.'

Chapter Twenty
Alice's malice

'Hell's bells, Alice! You're the dizzy limit,' Sally heard Rachel exclaim frustratedly on her first shift back at work.

'What? All I said was that I wonder how many calories there are in sperm. What is wrong with that?'

Rachel rolled her eyes in a hostile manner as she caught Sally's eye.

'You are at work, for heaven's sake! You are supposed to maintain the facade of being a professional! I don't want to hear about you partying all night, ignoring your child! I don't want to see you stealing hospital supplies before you go home! Try growing up!' Rachel hissed before marching off, shaking her head furiously as though beyond exasperated.

Sally checked the patient allocation book, hoping Alice had not been allocated a ventilated patient.

'What a bitch!' Alice blurted, unfazed by the accuracy of the torrent of insults.

She barely had time to think before others rallied to Rachel's defence.

'It's not too much to ask, that when you accept a professional wage, you behave in a professional manner,' Dr Jenny commented. 'None of your peers want their reputations tarnished by working with you, Alice. Aren't you concerned? In the UK, a nurse like you would have been performance managed with monthly reviews by now.'

'I don't give a rat's crack as long as I get paid,' Alice responded, frostily.

'That's obvious. Have some pride in what you do! Have some consideration for your colleagues! Develop some self-respect!' Jenny demanded assertively.

'Seriously! What is your problem?' Alice furiously shouted, standing up defiantly and placing her hands on her broad hips.

'I'm happy to call security, Alice. I'll get them to inspect your bag every time you leave the unit while I'm at it,' Jenny retaliated unperturbed, not looking up from the patient's chart she was writing in. 'You don't have a friend in the place. The physios complain you don't do your routine cares. You are giving your ventilated patients nerve palsies from not repositioning them regularly. Your colleagues have had an absolute gutful of you justifying your inept performance. You're not even answering your own ventilator and monitor alarms.'

Attempting to find an ally, Alice turned to Sally.

'Don't look at me to defend you, Alice. I have just needed two weeks off for the scalding you inflicted on me!'

Alice screwed up her face viciously. 'When I went to drop in and see how you were doing, Greg's car was parked out the front.'

'Yes, Greg and his parents brought my car back from the hospital. I would prefer you indulged in less partying before you come to work rather than delivering elaborate excuses,' Sally persisted.

'His car was there all night, Sally!' Alice insisted, keen on humiliation.

'Well, I would hardly be partying with a burnt groin, now would I, Alice!' was Sally's gut reaction. Clearing her throat, she sighed deeply before confessing. 'I am diabetic, so Greg offered to help me monitor my sugar levels and insulin while I was drowsy from painkillers. I needed help to do my dressings and a reminder to take my antibiotics. This conversation is not about me, Alice. It is about your colleagues demanding you lift your game!'

'Well, Greg should have taken me up on my offer. He would have got more action with me any day,' Alice smirked in a derogatory manner.

Sally pursed her lips at Alice's sheer audacity before a reddened blush stained her cheeks.

'Alice is lower than a snake's belly, Sally. She displays no empathy or compassion. Alice feels *sooo* entitled. Don't you, Alice?' Jenny goaded.

Outnumbered and failing to win any battles, Alice stormed off to her patient's bed area to get handover.

'How are you going now, Sally? Are the burns all healed?' Jenny enquired.

'Yeah, not too bad. I'm much better than the last time you saw me.'

'I'm glad to hear that. If you need any areas checked, just give me a shout,' Jenny offered.

Using her feet to roll the desk chair closer towards Sally, Jenny talked more softly. 'Are you and Greg an item, then?' Jenny smiled reassuringly.

'Greg asked me to date him after the Sydney ICU conference. We haven't even been able to go out yet.'

'But you like him, yeah?'

'Yeah.' Sally blushed.

'Go, girl!' Jenny nudged her enthusiastically. 'He's absolute eye candy! Alice has been flirting with him for months. He's as disgusted with her as much as everyone else is. You have no competition there.'

'I could not have recovered so well without his help. Without Greg, I would have had to go to my doctor's surgery to get the dressings done every day. Greg ran me a salt bath twice a day, then did the dressings afterwards too. He's been fabulous.'

'It has been amusing to watch,' Jenny said provocatively.

'What has?'

'Greg. He has been smitten with you! He's been desperately trying to get your attention for months. Alice has been salivating after him at work parties as though she is on heat. It was hilarious. Greg kept seating himself with other staff on either side of him so she could not make moves on him. Alice has been totally oblivious of Greg's attraction to you, until now, apparently. She kept drinking heavily while trying to flirt.'

Sally laughed. 'Oh, I see. That would have been funny to watch. Greg can't stand either her morals or her lack of work ethic.'

'Greg always sat watching the door, hoping you would arrive. When you did not come after a few hours, he would leave early.'

'Well, on my next days off, we will be finally able to enjoy our first date.'

'Ah, the joys of a new spring romance,' Jenny sighed, theatrically patting her heart in jest. 'You have chosen well.'

'Yes! While both of us were initially wary about the potential problems of a work romance, we are now motivated to make it work.'

'There's a little blonde nurse in the surgical ward who keeps wandering down here to get medications. She's also going to be disappointed. Even though Greg told them both he was taken, neither had backed off.'

'He is definitely taken! Do you think Alice was following Greg, or was genuinely worried about me?'

'I know I shouldn't admit this, but I saw Alice look up Greg's address on the computer. A few days later, she made a derogatory comment to the staff in the unit about him still living with his parents. Believe me, Greg was taken off the market at least five months ago, honey! You just didn't know it.' Jenny smiled, entertaining herself further by teasing the blushing Sally.

'Greg's more than just good looks, let me tell you. When these burns heal up, I am eager for the honeymoon phase,' Sally winked.

As Sally silenced the MET pager, Jenny grabbed the emergency pack, ready to head off to the rehabilitation ward event displayed on the screen.

On their return from the rehab emergency, the ICU team began their evening rounds just as Joe Stanley's drinking buddies arrived after their counter meals. Following his maggot infestation, Joe was successfully weaned off the ventilator but not yet awake and talking. Preserving Joe's modesty, Dr Jenny did a neurological assessment while his pub friends watched.

'We might need to do ammonia levels for liver failure,' the intensivist suggested when Joe remained drowsy and relatively unresponsive. 'Does he respond to painful stimuli?'

'We know how to test Joe's pain threshold,' his friends said.

'Your shout!' said one of his visitors loudly in Joe's ear while the other two folded over laughing.

Chapter Twenty-one
Lilly

*G*reg and Gordon returned home to find Lilly and Sally in the dining room with artificial silk flowers littering the table.

'What have you boys been up to?' Lilly asked enthusiastically.

'Just catching up with some new friends, Mum. They are coming around tomorrow on my last day off, if that is okay,' Greg responded.

'Oh, that's lovely, dear. Just don't forget – you need to be here for them, love, not at Sally's.'

'Yes, I definitely will, Mum. Are you free tomorrow too, Sally?'

'Yeah, I don't work until 7 pm tomorrow night.'

'Well, it's just your friend, Kylie, and her boyfriend, Taylor. Do you remember Taylor, the soldier whose father was in ICU?'

'Wait! Kylie is dating Taylor?'

'Yep, they are an item, aren't they, Dad?'

'Yes, they make an adorable couple actually,' Gordon replied distractedly, while analysing their meeting in his mind.

'How do you know more about my best friend than I do?' Sally enquired, keen to learn more details.

'Oh, I get around!' Greg taunted evasively.

'How is Jack doing?'

'He gets home today actually, after his physio. Taylor is not sure whether Jack might come too. They both don't want to leave him unattended.'

'The more the merrier, I say,' Lilly invited.

'Kylie plans to move into Taylor's room at their house when Taylor flies back to work.'

'Wow, a lot has changed while I was out of action,' Sally considered, looking intrigued.

'What will we get ready for your guests? Do you want pizzas?' Lilly suggested.

'Yes, pizzas and lasagne would be grand, Mum! Kylie hinted that old Jack loves lasagne. Well, actually, Kylie said that lasagne and caramel tarts would be his idea of heaven.'

*

The next day, Taylor, Jack and Kylie went to Greg's to meet their mother.

'This is my dad, Jack,' Taylor began as they entered the doorway. 'This is Greg, Gordon, Sally and ...'

'Lilly,' Greg announced, as his affectionate mother moved in for a hug. Her eyes were a brilliant turquoise green, accentuated by the jade shirt she was wearing over a mid-length, washed denim skirt that elegantly suited her.

'Pleased to meet you, Taylor. Come and take a seat,' Lilly said, pointing to the table and chairs behind her.

'Kylie, this is my mum, Lilly.' Greg continued. 'You have met my dad, Gordon. Dad, this is Taylor's dad, Jack.'

Jack tried not to lose his balance as he extended his bony thin hand towards them before slowly making his way towards the chairs.

'Hey, Kylie,' greeted Sally, bringing a plate of nibbles to the table. 'I heard some exciting gossip,' she teased, with her eyebrows elevated, looking mischievously towards Taylor.

'You heard right,' Kylie responded.

Pointing between Sally and Greg, Kylie retaliated with, 'Do tell!'

'All new,' Sally winked, offering cold and hot drinks. Taylor pulled out the chair ready for Jack, as he safely manoeuvred himself to sit.

'Does Kylie nurse with you two as well?' asked Lilly, keen to place everyone.

'No, Kylie and I go to university together. We both occasionally work for my dad,' explained Sally. 'We've been best mates for years.'

'And what do you do, Taylor?' Lilly enquired, looking up at his handsome face.

'I'm a soldier. I work out of town. I have to fly out again next Sunday.'

'Oh, that's a shame,' Lilly conceded.

'Yes, I've been home for two months while Dad was in hospital. When I fly out, Kylie is going to move into my room at home to look after Dad while I'm away. Dad's not long out of hospital. He's excited that all his hard work has paid off, aren't you?' Taylor said, placing his hands on Jack's shoulders. 'Dad was very determined to get home again.'

Jack nodded emphatically, a little breathless from his exertion.

'Well done, Jack,' Lilly said. 'I heard that you like lasagne.'

Jack looked gleefully at Lilly, grinning in agreement. 'I do, Lilly. I really do! These look delicious too,' he suggested, pointing to the caramel tarts.

'You dig in, Jack. Enjoy yourself,' said Lilly, popping a tart on a plate in front of him to save Jack getting up. 'I will put some in a box for you to take home.'

Jack rubbed his hands excitedly. 'I can see we are going to be good mates,' he laughed wickedly.

Trying to remember Lilly's name, Jack frowned temporarily. Losing his thought, Jack winked at Kylie and proceeded to bite into the tart, displaying not a shadow of guilt.

Although Taylor was simply content to meet his mother, his eyes followed her as Lilly fussed over their guests. Taylor observed the caring nature and fun-loving personality Greg had described. After learning about her fragile mental health, Taylor was totally impressed by his stepbrother's protective nature and his cohesive family unit. His mind wandered to the five crows at his house. Greg had seemed just as rapt at having a new brother too. The whole family had gone out of their way to be welcoming. Taylor tried to discreetly wipe away the tears welling in his eyes.

'Are you all right, love?' Lilly asked sympathetically, as she attentively served their guests.

'It is going to be very difficult flying back to work,' Taylor explained evasively. 'Dad's just out of hospital ... I have to leave my lovely new partner ...'

'I understand,' Greg empathised. 'We will have to send you some pics and emails of the good life. We will make sure we are all holding a beer, won't we, Dad?' he teased.

Taylor received the covert reassurance delivered: Greg, sensing his emotional turmoil, was hinting that photos and communication would be forthcoming. Taylor felt Jack's bony hand automatically rubbing his leg. It felt just like the day he'd first come off his bicycle. Kylie squeezed his hand in support from her side.

'So, we might need to have a beer together before you go,' Greg added. 'Are you allowed a beer, Jack?'

Jack looked at Kylie and winked. 'I don't know about

a full beer. Perhaps I could have just a glass out of my son's bottle.'

*

That night, recalling their wonderful gathering, Taylor broke down in Kylie's arms. His emotions were turbulently fluctuating with the excitement of having Jack returning home, his new intimate relationship and being delighted to meet his mother and brother.

Taylor had organised his flight to Sydney after a stopover in Brisbane. His biological grandparents had insisted they would meet him at the airport so that Taylor's time was not wasted in travel. Taylor had gone from being an only child to discovering he was now a member of a family of five and an extended family of ten, when he counted Timmy, Kylie, Sally and his biological grandparents. Kylie had even suggested that Taylor's maternal grandparents could stay at her flat on Taylor's next trip home, since they were both occupying Taylor's room at Jack's house.

*

'What did you think of Taylor, Mum?' Greg asked nonchalantly.

'What a lovely young man he is!' Lilly announced. 'It must be hard for him to go back to work after his dad has been so sick. He was pretty emotional, hey.'

'Dad and I wanted to talk to you about that, Mum. You know how you trust us to look after you, right?'

'Yes, Greg, you both do a wonderful job.'

'Well, I have some news for you,' Greg added, gently placing his arm around her shoulders.

'Bad news?'

'No, I think you will be pleased to hear it. It could be distressing, though.'

Lilly sat down, folding her skirt underneath her hands on her lap, listening intently. 'What is it? You and your dad look concerned.'

'As I told you this afternoon, I first met Taylor when Jack was admitted to intensive care.'

'Yes, that's right.'

'Then I met Taylor again in the shopping mall when I went to buy that suit to take Sally to the gala ball at the conference. Taylor was sitting on a seat, watching Kylie and Sally doing renovations at the mall for Sally's father.'

'Sally was doing renovations?'

'Yes, Sally and Kylie have always done some part-time work for Sally's father. He's a builder. They originally worked for Bill so as to get money for university; now the girls just do interior work if he needs a hand. Kylie's brother, Timmy, works part-time for Bill too when he comes home from university between semesters. At the moment, Sally's father has hurt his foot when he tripped over a tool that was carelessly placed. Anyway, I saw Taylor when he was sitting watching Kylie, and I was watching Sally.'

'I see.' Lilly nodded. 'Kylie and Sally are old friends, aren't they?'

'Yes, that's right. But I have some other news for you that may upset you.'

'Upset *me*?'

'Yes, you.' Greg looked at his father for support.

Gordon explained sensitively. 'I believe you will find it to be exciting news rather than bad news, Lilly. In fact, I think you will consider it good news. We just don't want to drop a big surprise on you suddenly and stress you out.'

'Okay ... You both look worried. Tell me what has happened?'

'We got a letter from the adoption people, Mum. The request was about your son wanting to meet you. Would you be interested in meeting him too?'

'Yes, definitely,' nodded Lilly, moving to the edge of her seat anxiously. 'You are both keen to meet him too, aren't you?'

'Yes, Mum. But Dad and I thought it might be better to go and meet him ourselves first. We wanted to meet him first to make sure you were safe. We also wanted to explain to him why his father's name wasn't on the birth certificate in case that upset him.'

'Oh, I see. How did he take that news?' Lilly looked curiously from one to the other.

Greg gathered up his mother's left hand in his, as Gordon reached for the other.

'When we told him, he was very caring. He was more

worried about your health, Lilly. He's a lovely chap. He was keen to meet you too,' Gordon elaborated.

'Oh, that's great!' Lilly beamed excitedly. 'When? Where?'

'We brought him around here today, Mum. It was Taylor. That was why he was emotional. Taylor was meeting you for the first time. Jack's got early dementia and is just out of hospital. So, Taylor did not tell Jack you were his biological mother. How do you feel about that news, Mum?'

'It's terrific news!' Lilly said, elatedly hugging them both and looking at them with pleading eyes. 'When can I see him again?'

'Would you like to go around and see Jack and Taylor tomorrow? They have invited us to Jack's house.'

'Yes! Yes! I would!' said Lilly eagerly, bouncing up and down in her seat.

'That's great, Mum! We will organise a time after Jack has had his bath and dressings done, say, about 1 pm. Taylor said it won't matter if Jack is still dozing after a big morning of activity. Sometimes Jack will nap until 2 pm.'

'Oh, yes! This is exciting! He seems such a lovely boy.'

'Yes, he does, Mum. Okay, we will organise that for you and take you. I don't work until tomorrow night, so we can both be there with you. Mum, would you mind not telling Jack? Taylor does not want Jack getting upset after he worked so hard to get out of hospital. Jack is still a bit weak. With his early dementia, Jack sometimes gets confused forgetting names.'

'Oh, I see ... I would dearly have loved to thank the people who raised my son.'

'You still can, Mum, but in other ways. Jack loves home-cooked meals. I can get a list of the foods he likes from Kylie, if you like. She is living around there in Taylor's room. When Taylor flies back to Sydney, Jack will go into a day centre while Kylie visits her other patients.'

'Jack could come here,' Lilly insisted.

'We could do that sometimes too, Mum. At the moment, Jack needs to continue his physiotherapy for his chest and exercises to keep his strength up at the day centre.'

'Ask Kylie what we can take around there tomorrow. I would like to make Jack, Taylor and Kylie something special,' Lilly announced.

'You probably won't see Kylie tomorrow, Mum. She will be working, but we will no doubt see them all again.'

'This is very exciting news, isn't it? Taylor is as handsome as you!' Lilly responded, giving Greg a strong hug. 'I see now why Taylor was so sad about going back to work.'

'Yes, Mum. Dad and I have had another thought, too. Tomorrow morning, while you are waiting to catch up with Taylor, we thought you might like to pick out some photos of us to email to Taylor. Then he will have some photos of us all to keep with him. We can send him some phone camera shots, too.'

'Oh yes! Yes! I'd like photos of Taylor growing up, too.'

'We might not be able to get those straightaway without alerting Jack, Mum. Taylor mentioned that if Jack sees any photos moved, he might panic about going into a nursing home. We will see if we can borrow some of his childhood photos to copy. Taylor might also snap some on his phone and send them to me. I will ask. I'm sure he will oblige us.'

'Wow, that's fantastic!' Lilly teared up. 'I hugged my other son today without knowing it!'

'Taylor knew, Mum. We discussed it all with him the other day when you were teaching Sally flower arranging. We went to meet Taylor while Sally stayed with you. Taylor did not mind meeting you for the first time, and us telling you later that he was your son. He did not want you to get upset. Taylor was very agreeable. He wanted the arrangement to be the least stressful for you as possible. Naturally we have to be careful what we say around Jack. Although Jack forgot your name the other day, Taylor says on most occasions, he is pretty astute.'

'Jack was lovely. We will have to make some lemon delicious tarts for that sweet tooth of his. Jack is such a darling!'

'Yes, Mum. Jack's wife, Michelle, died of bowel cancer a few years ago, I believe. My understanding was that the diagnosis was made too late. We won't talk about that in Jack's presence. He has short-term memory loss, but his long-term memory is still sharp.'

'I can't wait to see my other son again,' Lilly smiled excitedly. 'I am busting to see photos of his childhood. We should get Nanny and Pop here to meet Jack and Taylor.'

'Nanny and Pop are going to meet Taylor at Brisbane airport. Taylor has got two weeks' leave in January, so they are going to come here then. Nanny and Pop can either stay in my room or in Kylie's unit. She has invited them to use her place.'

'Oh, boy, I can't wait until tomorrow!'

'Until then, Mum, you can help us by looking through the photo albums and picking out some photos for Taylor. I will try to snap them on my phone and email them on to him, so Taylor can see them as a bigger size. You don't feel too stressed, Mum?' Greg asked cautiously.

'No, love! It's like you said – this is excellent news! We have finally met your older brother. The best bit is that we all like him and Jack.'

'Yes, our family has doubled in size with Sally, Kylie and Jack. Don't get upset if you cannot see Taylor at Christmas. We may be able to video call him, but I'm not sure. We might have to be content with catching up sometime in January when he comes home on leave,' Greg reminded her.

'We could invite Jack and Kylie over, though?'

'Yes, and Sally's family too, for Christmas, if you want.'

'Yes, we will. I can't wait until tomorrow to see Taylor again.'

'Let's pick out some photos for Taylor, honey,' Gordon

suggested, bringing over an album. 'Then we can sort out if you need to buy any ingredients for the recipes you want to make tomorrow.'

'What did you think when you first met Taylor?' Lilly asked, looking at Greg.

'I was absolutely impressed, Mum. Old Jack really loves his son dearly. He is totally devoted to Taylor, and that affection is genuinely returned. I could not help but like them both. Taylor feels torn between his work commitments and Jack becoming increasingly vulnerable. Taylor will be requesting more leave to come back in January.'

'It would be hard seeing Taylor so conflicted. I hope Taylor and Kylie will let us help them out a little with Jack. I want to thank Jack for raising Taylor in such a loving household.'

'We will try to visit regularly and see how we can help,' Gordon reassured, holding Lilly's hand for comfort.

Chapter Twenty-two
Jack

*A*ter all his physiotherapy exercises and hard-won battles breathing and separating from ventilator support, nothing soothed Jack more than a sleep in his own bed. He took a long nap before sitting outside in the sun to watch the spring flowers, bees and native birds. His life felt blessed again, particularly with Taylor staying home until the end of the week.

'I've got those groceries we discussed being delivered between ten and twelve, Dad,' Taylor announced.

'Good-oh,' Jack responded.

'Dad, would you mind us having some visitors around this arvy?'

'Visitors?'

'Yes, the friends you met yesterday with the lasagne and caramel tarts. Do you remember? Gordon, Lilly and Greg. Sally and Kylie will be working, but I would just like to catch up with them a few more times before I leave next Sunday.'

'Oh, yeah,' Jack looked up curiously.

'Yes, it will just be Lilly, Gordon and Greg Roberts,' Taylor said, looking for signs of recognition.

'Okay, well as long as you tend to your guests, that will be fine, son. I'm still struggling and a bit washed out, so I can't help you much at the moment.'

'That's no problem, Dad. They would just like to catch up with us again and say hello.'

'Okay. That's good, son. Are they coming after I have my bath? I'd like to look respectable for company.'

'Yes, around 1 pm, Dad, after your midday nap too.'

'Good plan, son.'

At 1 pm, Jack was still fast asleep after the exhaustion of his shower, ulcer dressing and lunch. As soon as they arrived, Lilly impatiently enveloped Taylor in a long embrace, only relinquishing him for Greg to follow up with a man hug. Gordon put down the food that Lilly had cooked to empty his hands for a handshake.

Lilly was soon diverted by the site of framed photos displayed on the lounge wooden buffet cabinet shelves. Taylor followed her over, showing her Michelle's photo.

'I always prayed that you would be looked after well,' Lilly confessed, studying the images.

'I was, without a doubt, well looked after. I had the best life imaginable with my parents,' Taylor emphatically reassured Lilly.

Jack smiled, overhearing Taylor's comments as he shuffled out of his bedroom.

'Taylor was always easy to get along with, unless there were electrical storms. He would literally jump out of his skin when the lightning cracked. Taylor had to sleep between Michelle and me then.'

Taylor left Lilly to keep looking at the photos, while he walked beside Jack, escorting him to the toilet, bathroom and then to a seat at the dining room table.

'What can I get everyone to drink?' Taylor asked.

When all declined a hot drink, Taylor opened the fridge door and passed out soft drink cans and juices, automatically filling up Jack's glass with sarsaparilla.

'Dad, look what Lilly has done!' Taylor exclaimed, putting a tray of lemon delicious tarts on the table.

Jack's face instantly lit up with pleasure.

'Kylie has told me what you like,' dobbed Lilly, placing a small tart on a plate within reach. 'Caramel tarts are number one, she said, with lemon delicious a close second.'

'Thanks, Lilly.' Jack leant forward, not delaying his first bite.

'And ... Lilly has brought over your favourite tuna mornay for tea, Dad!'

'You're the best!' exclaimed Jack, tapping both hands on the table to amplify his excitement. His eyes looked up and to the right, searching but unable to remember Lilly's name.

'Lilly will have you fattened up in no time, Jack,' reported Gordon, placing a hand on his own generous waist for illustration.

'I was just admiring the photos on your lounge cabinets, Jack,' Lilly commented. 'You have a lovely family.'

'You can bring them over if you want me to tell you about them,' Jack offered.

Lilly retrieved the picture of Taylor on a farm milking a cow. Jack told Lilly about their treasure hunt and the farmer attempting to catch the pirate bird with his shirt. Greg was just as rapt hearing about Taylor's childhood as Lilly was. Lilly returned the frame and selected another to bring over, a picture of Taylor on Michelle's knee, eating what looked like long rolls.

'Oh, I love that picture!' exclaimed Jack. 'Michelle and Taylor were cooking together. She had rolled and flattened out the biscuit pastry while she was waiting for the oven to warm up. Michelle and Taylor were using cookie cutters to make the biscuits into bunny rabbit, kangaroo and teddy bear shapes. Michelle turned around to wash her hands and lower the oven temperature, ready to put the biscuits in. When she turned back again, the tray of rabbits, roos and teddy bears were all cigars! Taylor had rolled the pastry in his little hands and put them back on the tray. So, we had cigars and cordial for our picnic.'

Lilly laughed. 'Greg used to roll his pastry dough into balls and eat it raw.'

'Our boys have both got themselves lovely partners

now, Jack,' Gordon declared. Unable to clear his full mouth, Jack nodded excitedly, his eyes creased in a grin.

'Kylie's puppy, Hayley, will come to live here soon, too, won't she, Dad?' Taylor reminded his father. 'We are just giving Dad more time to settle in after being in hospital. Hayley has been over for a few short visits, hasn't she?'

'Kylie is going to close her bedroom door of a night-time with Hayley inside, so that Dad does not trip or fall. Hayley is already spending a few hours more here every day to get used to this house.'

'The puppy has a lovely temperament,' Jack recalled. 'I can never remember her name, though. Taylor got a little fox terrier one Christmas when he was little. Since his puppy's coat was littered with brown and black spots, Taylor called him Freckles.'

'And Freckles used to dig tiny holes, all over the yard,' Taylor said. 'I remember Mum twisting her ankle in one at the clothesline.'

'And he slept in your room,' continued Jack. 'You made a bed for him in your dirty clothes basket, so he did not poop all over the carpet. Taylor had insisted on taking Freckles to school with him too, for "show and tell". He already had him in his school bag when we discovered his plan. Michelle put Freckles in his doggy carrier with a lead attached and went to school with Taylor, to bring him home after the talk.' Jack started laughing at the memory. 'His talk was about how much Freckles ate and pooped.'

They all enjoyed the afternoon reminiscing down

memory lane. Lilly and Greg hugged Taylor and Jack before departing, while Gordon settled for a firm handshake.

Chapter Twenty-three
Taylor's departure

*T*he morning Taylor was due to fly out from Toowoomba airport. He awoke heavy-hearted. He'd set his alarm for 5 am as he needed time to jog to rid himself of the gut-wrenching dread he felt. Taylor had always hated leaving Jack. This time, the trepidation was magnified by the trauma of leaving Kylie as well as his new extended family. He jogged in long strides for five kilometres until his heart slammed into his chest wall and his lungs tightened, leaving him breathing in heavy gasps.

As his shins tightened and his feet landed heavily on the concrete pathway, Taylor contemplated his career options. The only immediate decision made was to request more leave to return home after two months. However, he needed more time to decide if he would renew another five-year military contract when this current contract expired or whether he would try for a recruitment or training role that did not require overseas travel. His passion for travel and adventure was now replete. Taylor's desires had morphed into a need to spend more time with Jack, merging with his biological family and maturing his partnership with Kylie.

Taylor hoped the endorphins produced from his vigorous run would keep him calmer. For Jack, Lilly and Kylie's sakes, he was determined to avoid a tear-filled farewell. Yet he was already struggling to relax, especially after they had all insisted on seeing him off at the airport. Taylor wondered how the hell he would be able to endure all these goodbyes when he did not want to leave at all.

Jack had always been adamant about seeing his son off at the airport, ever since he was first recruited. The bottom line was that if the seventy-two-year-old Jack, not long out of hospital, was digging himself out of bed at 7 am, then Taylor could find all the grace and steely determination he could muster. Taylor was resolved to cover his distress with a plastic smile.

'Your friends are here, son!' Jack announced smiling, placing his arm on Taylor's for support. Jack recalled how his son had never enjoyed send-offs. Taylor had cried all the way to school on his first day as they walked along, even when Michelle had escorted him. For the first week of school, despite Michelle remaining with Taylor every day, he ran most of the way home in relief. Michelle had walked rapidly, struggling to keep their son in her sights. Michelle's funeral had been another extremely challenging moment for them both.

Taylor's resolve dissipated when he found Greg, Lilly and Gordon waiting near the dedicated luggage check-in area. Lilly instantly smiled before racing over enthusiastically to wrap him in a warm hug. The strength of her embrace suggested she knew he was emotionally distraught. Trying to maintain a calm facade, Taylor looked over her shoulder. Greg and Gordon had their heads together whispering with Kylie. They were passing a small black paper bag with string handles to her.

As Lilly released Taylor, Greg stepped in to greet him with another man hug and strenuous back pat. Jack looked up, concerned. He turned intuitively to Kylie, hoping she might distract his distraught son.

'This time, Taylor will be able to video call us every night, Jack,' Kylie intervened with a slightly raised voice. 'We both have cameras on our laptops, so I will be able to report all your mischief!'

Taylor looked at his thin, frail dad before his face was stricken with grief. Breathing out in a heavy sigh, Taylor looked distractedly over towards the check-in point, needing to make his escape.

'I'll just go and get processed,' Taylor said, excusing himself. The others waited to the side near the transit lounge, intent on trying to remain upbeat.

As Taylor joined them with his boarding pass, they

migrated slowly through the security checkpoints. Kylie and Jack sat either side of Taylor, with Greg, Lilly and Gordon facing them on the pale grey plastic chairs a metre away. Taylor looked down to find Jack's bony sinewed hands automatically patting his knee, silently helping him maintain his composure, as he always had. When he heard the boarding of his flight number announced on the overhead speakers, Taylor bit his lower lip as his emotions began to crescendo. Taylor gave Jack a final hug as tears began spilling over his now burning lids. Lilly moved in for another tense hug and cheek kiss, soon followed by a final man hug from Greg. Gordon produced a firm handshake and smile. Kylie kissed him passionately and melted into him, as Taylor peered down with a distraught sodden face.

'I'm going to miss you all so much,' Taylor said as his quivering chin caused his voice to break.

'We've taken care of that,' Lilly said, mopping her own eyes with a soggy tissue. Lilly handed Taylor the black bag. 'This is from us all. You're not to open this until you are seated on the plane. Otherwise, the airlines might have to pour you into your seat.'

'Oh God, thank you! Thank you all so much,' sobbed Taylor. 'This is so hard. I must be losing my mettle.'

'Well, you have gained a large family instead, so that's an excellent trade,' whispered Kylie, using a final hug to elevate Taylor's spirits.

'Taylor's always been one of those boys who hated

goodbyes. Every time he leaves town, my boy still tries to get me to stay at home,' Jack validated.

'And he's never succeeded yet,' responded Taylor with a warm smile.

At the top of the stairs, Taylor turned to give them all a final wave and forced smile before entering the plane.

*

When Jack returned home, he shuffled faster than usual directly towards his treats drawer. He laughed, coughed and spluttered at finding it stuffed to the brim with individually wrapped chocolates.

'I love my boy! Kylie! Come and take a look at this!'

Kylie laughed, witnessing the sight of Jack's treats drawer stuffed to capacity.

'That was a stressful departure, wasn't it, Jack? Shall I put the kettle on?'

Kylie walked to the front door on hearing the doorbell chime. Jack sat down at the kitchen table, assuming it was probably Taylor's friends from the airport visiting. His eyes were creased through his dark-rimmed glasses, but he looked up in delight as Kylie walked in holding a large bouquet of orchids, roses and baby's breath flowers in a white china vase.

'Look at this, Jack! Aren't they beautiful?'

He stood up to smell them before Kylie placed them in a vase in the middle of the dining table. Jack ran his soft hands over the base of the vase, admiring the contoured colourful image of the kookaburra featured there. Taylor had remembered Kylie mentioning her belief that the kookaburra was her power animal and spiritual guide. He thought the bird really did capture her cheerful bubbly personality. Kylie's hands shook as she opened the card.

'I love you so much, sweetheart. Thank you for looking after Dad. I cannot wait to return 10 January, xxx lots of love and hugs, Taylor.'

*

A week later, when Kylie had bumped into Sally in the mall, she discovered that the Roberts had not long returned from the airport when an Australian wildflower arrangement had arrived addressed to Lilly. Taylor had chosen a magpie display for the base of her floral design to incorporate his power animal and spirit guide, since Lilly was a blood relative. The magpie nature also reflected his mother's ingenuity, intelligence and adaptability. Gordon and Greg had laughed when the flowers had arrived with a parcel addressed to them containing Australian gourmet beers. The message read: It was great to meet you all. Mum xxx, I will video call soon and see you all in person again on 10 January. I have enclosed some posh beers for Greg and Gordon ☺.

*

Taylor sat on the plane, flipping over the photos compiled by Gordon, Lilly and Greg. The attached card said that Kylie had purchased the photo album for the Roberts family to fill. Each photo contained small anecdotes and stories written in Lilly's neat cursive hand of Greg's childhood and their family celebrations. Taylor took particular interest in his grandparents' images, hoping he might recognise them when Violet and Paull Maikie arrived in the airport's coffee lounge.

The plane was now circling, and it jolted slightly as the wheels locked down in preparation for landing.

Chapter Twenty-four
Greg

*G*reg met Sally's parents the following Sunday. Sally looked gorgeous wearing a loose blue sundress and white sandals. She had texted her parents to warn them that she would be introducing them to her new partner, knowing they would want to exert extra effort in tidying their house before Greg arrived. Greg was curious to witness how this visit would play out.

'Mum, Dad, this my handsome Greg,' Sally said. 'Greg, this is Bill and Carol.'

'Pleased to meet you, Greg,' said Carol, moving in for a hug.

Greg recognised the mild, right-sided, residual facial weakness of the stroke she had had. Bill limped over, balancing awkwardly in his moon boot, stopping to transfer his walking stick to his left hand to facilitate a firm handshake.

'You look like you've been in the wars,' Greg acknowledged.

'Yeah,' Bill replied. 'Our new apprentice carelessly discarded a hammer in a thoroughfare at the building site. I tripped over the flaming thing and broke my bloody ankle. But it's that frustrating ligament damage now taking forever to heal.'

'Sorry to hear that,' Greg commiserated. Taking Sally's cue, neither she nor he said anything about her burns.

He was now grasping why Sally had needed to be so independent and stoic. Sally had not wanted her parents fussing about her own health, while they were already maxed out. Bill and Carol's conservative three-bedroom house also suggested their business was struggling. In contrast to the affluent builder images portrayed in the media, there were loads of stories about companies going bankrupt, not paying tradies and contractors. Even when their construction business had struggled, Sally maintained that Bill was proud of making it a priority to always ensure his contractors were paid. No wonder Sally was taking on the additional responsibility of sorting their bathroom after Carol's knee replacement.

'Any word on the bathroom tiles arriving?' Sally enquired.

'They shouldn't be too far away. We have paid a deposit on the glass fixture. They will manufacture it to specifications when the tiles are laid, after we can give them a final measurement. It's been a hell of a year, hasn't it?' Bill moaned, raking his thick wavy hair. 'If it was raining film stars, I'd be catching Lassie!'

'I'd prefer Lassie,' joked Greg, keen to lift their mood.

'Sally helps us out around her shifts when she can. I have a foreman minding the job sites too,' Bill conceded. 'Otherwise, I could have lost my whole business with these Covid supply delays and struggles to get qualified tradesmen and contractors. This foot injury was the final dizzy limit!'

There have been more "final straws" than you think, Greg thought, looking up at Sally.

'Well, if you need a lift with anything, just holler,' Greg offered. I have no experience in the building industry, but I am happy to lend an extra set of hands.'

'Will do, thanks, Greg. I feel helpless. I find myself prowling around the lounge, thinking about all the work I should be doing.'

'Life can be hideous, can't it?' Carol said, recognising how untethered Bill felt.

'Yes, this year has been utterly obscene,' admitted Bill, sounding depressed.

'And you two work together?' Carol questioned, ardently diverting Bill from his miseries.

'Yes,' Greg said. 'We're both nurses. Sally is more qualified and senior to me.'

Bill looked up at Greg, captivated at that news. 'Well, treat my daughter well is all I ask. She's been the best daughter a bloke could have.'

'He does, Dad!' Sally reassured them. 'You should see the big bunch of flowers I have at home from Greg and his parents.'

'Are they locals, Greg?'

'Yes, they are now; they were originally from Brisbane. Their names are Lilly and Gordon Roberts. Do you know them?'

'No, but we could try to get everyone together for a meal at Christmas if you like,' Bill suggested. 'Hopefully, we should have run out of calamities by then. I bloody hope there are no more dramas. I can't take much more!'

'As you can see, Greg, Bill does not do injuries well, especially when the building industry is struggling. We are just a small company with limited resources. Having to pay a foreman to step in removes one labourer on the site.'

'It won't last forever, Dad,' Sally consoled. 'Greg's parents have invited us all over to their house this Christmas holiday. Kylie's boyfriend, Taylor, and his family will be there too. Taylor is a soldier, so he can't get home until mid-January. They are hoping Taylor can be available to video call through on the day. Lilly and Gordon have a large outdoor barbecue area at the back.'

Carol said, 'Please accept their kind invitation. We need to celebrate surviving this year of turbulence. We're in shit shape here. Not hosting anything this year will be a blessing.'

'Yes, that would also leave us to concentrate on finally getting this bathroom sorted,' offered Sally.

Bill and Sally discussed the bathroom plans together, listing the consumables like hand grips and towel rails that had yet to be ordered.

'Why don't you leave it until I can give you a hand, Sally?' Greg volunteered. 'We could put in for four days off together.'

'Okay, thanks, I'd appreciate that,' Sally said gratefully.

'I'll be following your instructions, of course. You and your dad will be the brains of the operation.'

'Thanks, Greg.' Bill looked relieved.

*

When Greg returned to work and opened the roster folder to synchronise his next four days off with Sally's requests, he discovered a line drawn though Alice's name.

'Is Alice on holidays?' he asked Rachel.

'No, she finally got caught stealing hospital property when she left on her last shift. The security officer escorted her up to the business manager's office, then off the hospital premises.'

'Sacked?'

'No. Alice was apparently offered the choice of resigning, "effective immediately", to avoid charges being laid. She accepted the offer so that a criminal history would not be recorded to affect her nursing registration.'

'God knows, Alice had received plenty of warnings. We had all hoped she would simply lift her game.'

'I feel sorry for her daughter. Gemma is bonding to her grandmother because Alice never gives her any thought. I am concerned that Alice's employment termination will not buy Gemma any further attention. Gemma is Alice's last thought after her love life and partying. It's very sad, really. Alice still makes excessive demands on her mother, despite knowing her mother is diligently looking after her daughter. It saddens me to see Alice behave as though she feels like she is the only one worthy of attention. I know this sounds pathologically bizarre, but I'm concerned that Alice seems to perceive Gemma as her sibling. Alice actually competes with her daughter for her mother's attention.'

Greg frowned with concern. 'Well, I hope Alice's mother lives a long life to protect that child.'

'Yes, me too,' Rachel responded. 'I heard that Alice is apparently applying for pharmaceutical sales representative positions that require a lot of travelling. Maybe Alice being away from her mother could be ideal. No patients would be at risk, and the daughter would have a safe role model.'

'I hope she gets roles that use her nursing qualifications but without requiring her to do patient care.'

'Me too. I would like to see Alice get counselling, though. Many of her behavioural patterns could be consistent with sexual abuse.'

'Oh, that's terrible! You mean ... like the sleeping around and excessive drinking?'

'Yes. I am convinced that Alice has been a victim of an early childhood sexual assault. I also wonder if that is why she is not bonding to Gemma. Gemma may have been a product of that assault.'

'Then I pray she gets the help she needs. It seems like we were all treating the signs Alice displayed rather than identifying the cause. Do you think you should mention this to the nurse unit manager? We would still advocate on Alice's behalf as long as she committed to long-term counselling.'

'Hmmm, it is just my suspicion after years of psychiatric nursing, but ... you're right. I should advocate for a colleague. Sometimes when people really piss you off, you get so distracted by their behaviours that you fail to analyse the cause. I am going to do that.'

'Another thought you've dropped in my head is whether the perpetrator could be a relative? I worry that Gemma could also be at risk.'

Rachel marched off to the nurse unit manager's office, determined to see if anything could be done to offer Alice counselling.

Chapter Twenty-five

The importance of
a living blood relative

*U*ntil meeting Taylor, Greg had not really considered any of the issues faced by adopted children. On his second shift after he'd returned to work, with Sally remaining on another week of sick leave, his new admission, Peta, changed all that.

Peta was admitted as an "indeterminate suicide attempt", as the circumstances surrounding her single motor vehicle accident were suspicious but unproven. The young lady had hit the only cluster of trees on a straight country road. Peta claimed that her nose had begun to run, that she had leant over to the passenger side of her car to get a tissue and abruptly lost control of her vehicle. However, Peta's distraught husband, Josh, contested his wife's statement adamantly. Josh claimed that Peta had begun drinking wine recently as a symptom of her depression.

Josh insisted that drinking alcohol was inconsistent with Peta's usual health-conscious behaviours, particularly considering she was wanting to get pregnant.

Josh was demanding psychological counselling for Peta, as he was concerned for her safety. According to the gynaecologist, there was no physiological reason that Peta could not become pregnant. Josh believed that having her own child was crucial to his wife's mental health as she was an adopted child. Josh had described Peta as being obsessive about wanting a known biological next of kin. The gynaecologist had suggested that Peta avoid shiftwork as the circadian rhythm disruption it caused was implicated in causing hormonal chaos and infertility issues.

'Peta placed a strong emphasis on having a biological family. She wants a living blood relative as next of kin,' Josh insisted. 'After being married for five years, at twenty-eight Peta's mood had plummeted into depression after her biological parents had declined to meet her. To make matters worse, Peta had not been able to use her pregnancy kit when her body kept cycling every month after three years without contraceptives.'

Greg empathised, wondering whether Taylor had experienced similar thoughts about wanting his own blood relative.

Chapter Twenty-six
The score card

A few weeks later, as arranged with his parents, Greg visited Sally for his evening meal on his way home from work. He was no sooner inside the doorway when the radiant Sally poured herself into his arms, moved onto her tiptoes and delivered a long seductive kiss. Before Greg realised it, his scrub shirt was being lifted over his head. A groan escaped his lips as Sally caressed her splayed hands over his solid, hirsute chest. Greg ran his hand under her hair to keep her pressed to his lips while his mouth devoured hers.

'I want you,' Sally whispered, 'so badly. You're becoming like an addiction. I now want more!'

'Ooh,' Greg gasped as his eyes ogled the flimsy, plum coloured, lacy negligee accentuating her feminine shape. The thin fabric, clinging to her feminine curves tantalised his imagination and caused a chemical storm.

Sally moved in for another long passionate kiss, as she simultaneously undid his trouser button. As Greg shucked off his clothes just inside the doorway, her tiny bare feet with shiny mauve toenails slid up his bare skin provocatively. Smugly satisfied with her success, Sally's eyes followed his every move.

Greg moaned, 'I'm not willing to wait any longer. I have thought about you all day.'

She kissed him and stroked his tongue through his open lips. Greg's lips migrated down to her throat and upwards to her earlobes. Sally pressed his mouth gently open, deepening the kiss.

'You have waited ever so patiently,' Sally whispered huskily in his ear, as she led him by the hand into the bathroom. When she stopped, her soft voice close to his ear turned him on.

Greg nibbled Sally's lower lip, allowing his tongue to sweep along her teeth. He brushed kisses over her neck with a hand at the back of her head. After drawing her into another long passionate kiss, Greg lifted Sally's night dress over her head to find her naked underneath.

'Now I am going to lather you *all* up,' she said, turning on the shower. Sally looked down blatantly, stimulating him at every opportunity. Greg's eyes shut as their sexual tension built. His breathing became ragged, trying to restrain his impulses as the sweet torture of Sally's naked body melted into his. The way Sally provocatively played with his chest hair was the epitome of temptation. Her rough hands caressed his nipples with a feather touch that left his heart hammering in his chest. Sally's rough hands wandered, as though memorising his athletic torso, before she began nuzzling his nipple into her mouth. Greg's gaze took in her slim legs, her tiny firm waist and pert nipples, as sizzling chemistry and electricity arced between them.

Greg smoothed his fingers over her jaw back and forth in a move that was both rhythmic and sensual. He perceived an eagerness in her that was desperately waiting to be sated. With the warm water running, they both stepped into the shower. Sally's rough hands wandered over, circling and soaping his broad virile chest. The fresh scent of roses lingered on his skin in the steamy shower as her rough hands navigated the corrugations of his spinal vertebrae. Her hands slid over his shoulders and down his back to his narrow hips, enjoying their tactile adventures.

'Hmmm, you have a sexy toned butt,' Sally complimented, using her hands to move his pelvis suggestively towards her. Greg's hardness left her in no doubt she was having the desired effect, as her touch and scent overpowered him.

For the first time ever, Sally's firm breasts cushioned his chest, leaving Greg longing for more. His erection strained against her. Greg soaped her breasts, circling his hands around and over her smooth slender back. His hands wandered over her soft bottom, and around to her front as he continued his exploration.

'Hmmm, let's take this into the bedroom,' Greg moaned.

Sally shivered as his tongue circled her nipples. Her eyes displayed raw lust.

Still saturated, Greg carried Sally to the bedroom. Sally lay on top of him on the bed, supporting her weight on her elbows as their urgency grew. After so many weeks of intense longing, she sat on him, gyrating him into a frenzied release. Greg's hands released her breasts as his body arched backwards, spent. Sally shuddered before collapsing limply on top of him.

Greg rolled onto his side, holding Sally for another longing kiss, relishing her sexual rosiness. She looked totally gratified.

'Your mum is not expecting you home tonight. I told her we were going to have pizza and movies.'

'Hmmm, I am certainly enjoying this channel ... Hell!' Greg suddenly sat up in alarm. 'I forgot to wear a condom!'

'It's all fine,' Sally replied, unperturbed. 'When you said you wanted a long-term relationship, I got a contraceptive script with my medical clearance,' Sally whispered, with her tongue sensually following the contours of his ear.

'Oh ... that's good. I was not focused on anything but you. You had me feeling so urgent for relief I could only think of being inside you.'

'Good. You were very patient. You don't need to be anymore.'

'You invigorate every nerve in my body. Every time I am around you, I crave your touch.'

'And now I'm all yours.'

Greg moved closer, relishing her soft breasts firmly resting on his chest as he pashed Sally longingly.

'I really do love you, Sally Price.'

Greg raked his fingers tenderly through her curly bangs. As he released them, the curls resumed their springy shape.

'It seems like we have both waited for this moment for ever. I love you, too.'

Sally began massaging a scented lotion over Greg's still damp chest. She rubbed the lotion on his limbs, stroking upwards towards his heart.

'Hmmm, have you been scheming all day, sexy Sally?'

'Hmmm, yes. I wanted to make this moment a most memorable experience for you.'

'Well, it certainly has been that!'

'You're my toy now,' Sally whispered daringly. 'I restore my toys. They're never discarded.'

Sally gave him butterfly kisses before her tongue circled his nipples. Greg began losing control as Sally's firm breasts pressed enticingly skin to skin against him, igniting him for a second pairing.

When she'd finished rekindling Greg's appetite, she lay dozing with her head on Greg's chest.

Chapter Twenty-seven
Jack's endless love

*K*ylie was running late. Her last community client had experienced a bout of chest pain, just as she was about to leave to collect Jack from the day therapy centre. After administering her sublingual nitrate tablet, and commencing her home oxygen, Kylie needed to remain for a further thirty minutes to ensure she was okay. Since Lilly and Gordon had often volunteered to look after Jack, Kylie rang to see if they could bring him home and wait with him until she arrived. Kylie was yet to do a final check on her unit on the way home, with Timmy due to return back from university any day now. Kylie hadn't worried about that so much, because she had planned to go there on the way home, after picking Jack up.

Lilly and Gordon happily helped Kylie out of her predicament by transporting Jack home; Lilly put the kettle on to make Jack a cup of tea. Jack was in his usual high spirits. Lilly grew concerned when Hayley had not ventured out to greet them. She went searching to make sure Kylie's puppy was safe, only to find her snoozing among her toys in her bed in Taylor's room. On the way back to the kitchen, Lilly automatically stopped at the mantelpiece, to once again admire the Robinson family photos.

'You should be very proud of your son,' Jack told the surprised Lilly.

'I am ... proud ... of *both* my sons,' Lilly honestly replied. 'How did you know?'

'Taylor could not stop watching you and Greg in particular.' Jack nodded approvingly. 'I am glad you have all been reunited. I was desperate for Taylor not to be left alone when I die. Now I'm relieved he won't be. Thank you for giving Michelle and me the pleasure of raising your boy. He made our family complete. Michelle always wanted children. When we married, I did not know I could not have them.'

Jack's confession was followed by a bout of his hacking cough.

'Thank you for raising him, Jack. You did an amazing job. You and Michelle should be proud of all you have achieved. He is such a well-mannered, loving, considerate young man,' Lilly confirmed.

She was constantly amazed at Jack's absolute faith and seemingly endless capacity to love. He displayed no bitterness or resentment at their intrusion into his life. Jack was just one of those endearing gentlemen who simply wanted Taylor to be loved.

'Turquoise eyes are very rare, Lilly. You put a jade, light blue or purple shirt on Taylor and his eyes will turn exactly the same colour as yours,' Jack smiled. 'Are ... you his father?' he asked curiously, frowning while trying to remember Gordon's name.

'No, I met Lilly three years after Taylor was born. Lilly has bipolar disorder, Jack. She got very unwell and developed a psychosis in her teenage years before the condition was diagnosed. So, we don't know who Taylor's father is.'

Lilly elaborated. 'During my teenage years, Jack, when I got pregnant, my bipolar disorder had not been diagnosed or treated. I was in a manic psychosis when I got pregnant, apparently. I was so ill I'm afraid I have no idea who Taylor's father was because of the illness, and I remember very little of the pregnancy. I virtually have very little memory of almost two years of my life. My condition was really unstable. When you are psychotic, you have no concept of reality, so it was not a safe place to raise a baby. My pregnancy was also affected by the limited drugs that I could be safely prescribed for the baby's health. At the time, my parents had a full-time job getting my mental illness stabilised, and they could not manage both me and my baby. Eventually my parents helped me to get my life on track again. Gordon is my carer, and Greg helps too. When I change from the manic to the depressive phases of this condition, the medications need to be adjusted as soon as possible.'

'Well, let me be honest and tell you that Greg is an amazing kid,' Jack complimented, 'and you are both amazing parents.'

'Thank you, Jack.' Lilly teared up, automatically putting her arms around Jack's bony shoulders to comfort him. 'I don't know how I can ever repay you for the kindness and love you gave to my boy.'

'The love he reflected back to us daily was its own endless reward. He loves you, Greg and Gordon too; otherwise, he would never have invited you here. Taylor has grown into such a compassionate, socially aware young man.'

'Yes, he most definitely has. It was funny how Taylor and Greg met when you were admitted to Intensive Care, hey. Almost like divine intervention, as Kylie would say,' Lilly said, smiling affectionately.

Jack inhaled deeply after recovering from another coughing fit.

'I honestly don't know how they copy photos these days, with the Kodak company not around anymore. But you are quite welcome to borrow any of the pictures here that you like. Lilly, if you can bend down to that bottom drawer there,' Jack indicated, pointing to a varnished timber cupboard, 'there are several albums we can work our way through, if you like.'

Lilly keenly retrieved the top album for Jack to recall Taylor's childhood stories and funny antics for her.

Looking at his cute little face, Lilly remarked, 'Taylor's so handsome, I was surprised that he has remained single, until recently.'

'Taylor was engaged.' Jack wiped a tear from his eyes with his handkerchief before continuing. 'His lovely fiancée, Heidi, was killed in an accident. Taylor was so devastated afterwards that he isolated himself for years. It was so tragic. Heidi was such a lovely girl. She was killed about eighteen months after Michelle passed away from cancer. But he has both Kylie and her brother ... err ... err ... Timmy now.'

Chapter Twenty-eight
Everyone home

With Gordon and Lilly now spending a few hours with Jack, Kylie dashed to her unit. She parked her car closer to the stairs to carry up the grocery bags of fresh fruit, vegetables, milk, bread and butter to stock up the fridge. Unlocking the door and entering her unit, Kylie discovered a tall brunette wearing a towel, making her way down the hallway to Timmy's room.

'Sprung badly,' Kylie laughed, greeting Timmy in his boxers. Timmy's eyes lit up in amusement.

'Guilty as charged, sis!' Timmy laughed before turning to introduce his favourite women to each other. 'Joanne, this is my big sister, Kylie. Kylie, this is the amazing student teacher I met in the library.'

'Looks to me like you've been studying anatomy, bro,' Kylie taunted.

Joanne blushed instantly and dropped her head as

Timmy greeted his sister with a hug.

'Welcome, Joanne. I am very pleased to meet you.'

'You, too,' replied Joanne, exiting briskly with a quick wave. 'I am going to dash in and get dressed.'

Joanne shyly retreated with her wet hair dripping onto her bath towel.

'I am busting for you both to meet my partner, Taylor,' shared Kylie. 'He will be home after Christmas, about 10 January.'

'Wow, sis.' Taylor flexed his hands rhythmically. 'Come on, we need pics!'

Kylie swiped to unlock her phone. 'This is Taylor,' Kylie announced cheerfully.

'Lordy, look at the size of him,' Timmy gasped, 'He's a man mountain!'

'Taylor is solid muscle. And this is his dad, Jack ... and this is his brother, Greg. Greg dates Sally now.'

'Blimey, it's like you've inherited a whole family!'

'Will you and Joanne be around for Christmas? They have all been talking about having a big barbecue, with Sally, Greg and Taylor's families all present. You and Joanne are invited too. Taylor won't be home until January, but we are hoping he might be able to video call in.'

'I'll have to check with Joanne's parents. I'm not sure what they are doing yet.'

'Of course. How is uni going?'

'Joanne and I both like primary school teaching, so we are enjoying our subjects and often study together.'

Joanne re-emerged from Timmy's room, looking slightly flustered.

'Joanne, would you like a coffee, tea or juice?' Kylie offered.

'An apple juice would be lovely, if you have one, thanks,' she timidly replied. Kylie poured them all drinks.

'Would you like Hayley to come back here while you are home? She's missed you, let me tell you.' Kylie smiled, trying to put Joanne at ease. 'Or you're both welcome to come and visit her at Jack's.'

'We might come and see Hayley at Jack's tomorrow, if that's okay. I am going out to meet Joanne's parents.'

'Are they in town here, Joanne?'

'Not far away. They live about ten kilometres out towards Dalby on a rural property. Timmy is coming mustering with us before he helps Sally, Bill and Greg with their bathroom renovations next week.'

'That's lovely. Well, I'm going to have to head back to Jack's now. Nice to meet you, Joanne. I'll see you both tomorrow.'

'Yes, you too.'

'See you tomorrow, bro,' Kylie said, kissing Timmy's cheek. 'I was not sure if you were arriving today or tomorrow, so I tried to stock up the fridge a bit.'

'Thanks, sis.'

'If you can't do Christmas, please don't forget to keep 10 January free if you can. I'd like you both to meet Taylor.'

'I know a Jack and a Taylor. Their last name was

Robinson,' Joanne said.

'You do?'

'Yes, they used to come to our family farm when we were little. Michelle and Jack were close friends with my parents.'

'Oh, that's great. It will be great for Jack to catch up with old friends. You must see if your folks are free for 10 January too. I'll have to clear an invitation with Lilly and Gordon, but I am sure your family will be most welcome. They both love to cook!'

'I could talk to Mum and Dad about Jack and Taylor coming out to the farm again too, if you like. It's been years.'

'I'd be happy to drive Jack out there one weekend.'

'I can't wait to see Taylor again. I still remember us teaching Taylor to drive a tractor. He learnt very quickly. Mr and Mrs Robinson nearly had a heart attack when Taylor was driving the tractor up a hill and the lighter front end began lifting up. We forgot to tell Taylor to reverse up slopes. Taylor called me Jo-Jo. He used to swing me on a rope swing with a tyre seat.'

'You're not the children they did their treasure hunts with?'

'Yes. The Robinsons did treasure hunts with us. How did you know?' Joanne asked, gobsmacked.

'Taylor was telling me about your dad taking off his shirt to catch the pirate bird,' Kylie laughed, wholeheartedly relaying the full story for Timmy.

'Jack's always been as thin as a whip, for all the treats he puts away,' Joanne grinned. 'Their visiting seemed to taper off after Michelle and Heidi died. They both just seemed so sad.'

'Jack is still thin.' Laughing, Kylie added, 'and he's still a sugar junkie.'

*

On 10 January, Taylor returned home to stay. His submission of an application to transfer to the Brisbane barracks had been accepted, and Jack was elated. Taylor told Jack and Kylie that his mind and body were telling him that Brisbane was where he needed to be. After his month of annual leave was finished, Taylor would be travelling home from Brisbane to Jack and Kylie nearly every weekend. He would be driving his new grandparents to and from Brisbane on a few of those trips as well. They had kept in regular contact after their first meeting, and Taylor had dined with them at the airport on his return flight to Brisbane.

Taylor and Jack's social network was expanding, and Kylie and Timmy were getting used to the novel experience of being members of this growing family. At their Christmas party, they had all decided to delay their present opening until Taylor arrived home. Kylie had made Taylor a bird feeder and bird boxes to install in the large mango tree in Jack's back yard. Taylor gifted

Kylie a beautiful dress that Lilly had picked out during a video call. Greg got Sally a holiday to Tasmania and Bill, Carol, Sally, Kylie and everyone else put in money for accommodation expenses to encourage Joanne and Timmy to have a car trip up the coast to Cairns during their next semester break.

At their January barbecue, Jack and Taylor were introduced to Bill and Carol and reacquainted with Joanne's parents. Greg and Gordon had waited until Taylor, Jack, Bill and Timmy arrived before opening the gourmet beers Taylor had bought. While the whole family lazed around relaxed and enjoying their smorgasbord, Jack was filling up on Lilly's condensed milk tarts. Lilly was particularly excited to be seeing more of Taylor.

Kylie and Taylor, Greg and Sally, Timmy and Joanne – it was the first time but not the last for the three new couples to be together.